PROVEN WAYS TO THE TOP

125 Great Strategies to Increase Your Productivity

By

MARC SILVERMAN

MBA, CLU, ChFC, CFP Practitioner

Standel Publishing

Proven Ways To The Top

Silverman Financial and the Securities America companies are unaffiliated.

Published by Standel Publishing

First printing. Printed in the United States of America 2010
Second printing 2014

Cover art by Ken Harris Graphic Design

ISBN 978-0-9845581-1-7

Dedication

I dedicate this book to my best friend and wife Patti, and to Cara—the best daughter a father could have. They make everything I do more worthwhile—and a lot more fun.

Introduction

Selling financial services is a difficult profession. It requires the advisor to manage several functions at the same time. They have to be great prospectors. Then they have to be incredible listeners. Once they have the facts, they need to be architects and craft an ethical and technically correct solution. Then it has to be administered properly and implemented. These are all skills that require training and experience.

Marc has reached into his bag of tricks and pulled out 125 ways advisors can increase their productivity and improve their marketing and brand. These ideas are time tested and proven to work. They are not theories or concepts a home office staff person has thought up in a think tank. They are the real deal. Anyone with initiative and creativity can take these ideas and put them to work immediately.

As most in the business know, Marc is an accomplished professional. His years of experience and expertise qualify him as one of the top advisors in the country. Not only does Marc's sensational production demonstrate his effectiveness, but it speaks volumes about the ideas and strategies which he discloses in significant detail in this book. He has revealed the heart of his success and the best ideas he has that you can use to achieve similar results.

Thomas Edison once said that "Genius is one percent inspiration and ninety-nine percent perspiration." If that is true, then Marc is a genius. His perspiration and hard work in the early years led him to the wisdom and clarity he has today. Fortunately for us, he has synthesized it into this book, *Proven Ways to the Top* which includes 125 ideas every financial advisor can learn and apply.

Marc reveals the struggles he endured in his early years and how the lessons he learned brought him to the place he is today. He shares the methods he used successfully in the beginning to grow his practice and the diligence he applied to track his success. Anyone who masters his simple and common sense solutions can achieve their goals and attain success.

Marc is very candid in this book. He has spelled out how he grew his business and why he shifted markets, even though he was very successful. He values his time and the benefits of repeatable (retention) income. By building a clientele of income-oriented clients, he has done both—expanded his time and stabilized his income.

This book is NOT just about selling annuities to the senior market. This book is about the value of systems, processes and accountability. So regardless of what market an advisor wants to serve or develop, there are ideas and tools for everyone. I got a lot out of the book and I have been in the business *only* 45 years.

I remember when John Prast, executive director of the Million Dollar Round Table and I had the good fortune to visit Marc in his office in 2009. Marc gave us a tour and showed us some of his memorabilia, specifically, all of his records dating back to his first year in the business. He pulled out one of them and showed us how he set goals and kept himself accountable. His records were meticulous and there for anyone to see. At the same time, he showed us his business systems and processes. How he treats clients and in general told us how he had learned to build a business instead of just being a salesperson selling policies. It was fascinating and very educational.

John told him he should write a book. He should put down all of his ideas and share them with others who are trying to find their niche and their rhythm in the business. Marc said he would think about it. Well, think about it, he did. And here is the result. *Proven Ways to the Top* is the product of his incredible creativity and productive mind.

This book is truly a gift to anyone who reads it. Study this book. Learn from it and apply what fits your personality and practice. There is something here for everyone. I am confident Marc's contribution to the body of knowledge sought by most agents will benefit many for years to come. They are timeless ideas and the best part is they are practical and easy to implement. I would be surprised if an advisor took just 10 of these ideas and put them into use that they would not see a significant increase in their production within 6 months.

Try and prove me wrong. Hope you benefit as much as I did.

It was a privilege to work with Marc on this book. His history and experience parallel what many other great producers have learned and shared over the years. I truly believe this book can be a turning point in the career of many advisors who struggle with prospecting and process. Marc's talent for simplifying and relating what he has learned is a valuable contribution to the industry.

Guy Baker, MBA, MSFS, CLU

Table of Contents

Who Is Marc Silverman, and Why Am I Writing This Book? 1
How Is Success Defined? 5
My First Professional Insurance Experience 7
Why a Book? 12
Starting Out 14
Keeping In Touch 16
Review Old Calendar Books 17
No Doesn't Necessarily Mean No 18
Why Stay Involved In Study Groups? 19
Pick a Specialty and Do It Well 20
Getting Out of Life Insurance 22
Target Marketing 23
Know Your Product and Know It Well 24
Not Everyone's Yes Means the Same Thing 25
Making Phone Calls 27
Tracking Your Numbers 29
Keeping Records 30
What Kinds of Records are Important? 31
Stay Disciplined 32
Goal Setting 33
Three Levels of Income Goal Setting: Conservative, Realistic and Aggressive 34
The One Card System 36
Never Give Up 37
Personal and Professional Goals 39
The Month of December 40
Get a Mentor 41
Sales Results Book 43
Track Your Calls 44
Strategic Relations 45
Farm Club 46
Prospecting 47

The $2 Bill 49
Direct mail 51
Block of Wood Concept 52
Personal Observation 54
The Harder I Work the Luckier I Get 57
Client Appreciation 58
Love Affair Marketing 59
Other Marketing Ideas 60
Hire Staff and Delegate the Role of Appointment-Making 61
Invest In People to Help You 64
EZ Data 67
Don't Count on Your Memory 68
Statements of Understanding 69
The Little Details Make a Big Difference 70
Answer By the Second Ring 71
Promote Your Staff to Key Positions 72
Follow Through and Follow Up 74
Create To-Do Lists 76
Hire Knowledgeable People 77
Rationale for Hiring a Marketing/
Lead-Generating Person In Your Office 78
Using the Web 79
Referrals 80
Referral List 82
Ask Around 83
Unparalleled Service 84
Be Passionate 85
50 Hours Per Sale = a Successful Insurance Sales Professional 86
Prospect Where You Play 87
Centers of Influence 88
Get Involved In Industry Activities 90
Words of Tony Gordon 91
Find a Financial Planner Better Than You and Become Friends 92
Marketing Your Business 93

Get Your Name Out There 94
Target Marketing 95
Workshops 96
Sell Yourself 97
How to Develop Workshops 98
When to Hold a Workshop 99
What to Talk About 101
How to Get Them to Come 103
What to Serve and Not Serve at a Workshop 105
What to Wear 106
Who Attends From the Office? 107
How Many Should You Invite? 108
Pay Attention to Length 109
Using a Projector 110
Give Everyone Name Tags as They Enter the Workshop 111
Connect With the Audience 112
Pass Out Materials 113
Provide a Questionnaire 114
Get Guest Speakers Involved 115
Follow Up With the Audience 116
Be Different 117
Compensate Your Staff for Helping at Workshops 119
Inject Humor Into Your Workshops 120
Get Your Workshop Compliance Approved 121
How to Take Advantage of Continuing Education Requirements 122
Serve the Masses, Eat With the Classes 124
Bring a Friend 125
Fewer but Better Qualified 126
Key Ingredients for Sales 127
Get Them Into Your Office 128
Make a Commitment 129
Sending Flyers 130
Plan Workshops In Advance 131
More on How to Sell Yourself Through Workshops 132

Have the Home Field Advantage When You Have a Meeting 134
What are You Trying to Accomplish? 136
Where to Hold a Meeting 137
Make It a Comfortable Environment 138
Decorating Your Office 139
Display Thank-You Letters 141
Dress Code 142
Give Clients Things They Like 143
Bake Cookies 144
The Audio Business Card 145
Love Affair Marketing 146
Network Your Clients 147
Referral Sources 148
Make Thank-You Calls and Send Thank-You Letters 150
Remember Their Birthdays 151
More About Birthday Phone Calls 152
CardWare 153
Advertise Yourself 154
Market Through Your Web site 155
Ice Cream Day and Picnic 156
Employee Handbook 157
Annual Client Reviews 158
Always Keep In Contact 159
Prospecting Via CD Due Dates 160
It Doesn't Always Go Right 161
Dictation Services 162
How I Do It 163
Know Your Revenues and Expenses 165
Know Your Ratios 166
Read Books by Motivational Speakers 167
Get Going! 168
Appendix 169

Are You Committed to Success?

Are you 100% dedicated to building a bigger, more profitable business and want to know how to work harder and play harder? Are you ready to experience less frustration, be more highly organized, earn more income, and want to learn marketing and prospecting secrets that really work?

If so, then read on, because I learned how to do exactly that with the strategies and techniques that follow—and I'm ready to share my success with you.

CAN YOU ANSWER THESE SIMPLE QUESTIONS?

1. Do You Have a Vivid Mental Picture of What You Want Your Career and Income to Be Like?
2. Do You Have an Achievable Financial Goal for Your Financial Planning or Insurance Business?
3. Have You Committed Your Business Strategy to Paper?
4. Do You Know How to Eliminate Counter-Productive Practices?
5. Are You Spending More Time Planning Your Summer Vacation Than Mapping Out Your Professional Future?
6. Do You Know Exactly How You're Going to Get From Where You Are to Where You Want to Be?

Who Is Marc Silverman, and Why Am I Writing This Book?

I am originally from Toronto, Canada. I was born August 17, 1959. I attended the University of Toronto and then transferred to the University of Miami.

While I was growing up, I was surrounded by incredibly successful friends who came from fairly well-to-do backgrounds. I had no patience as a young man and there's a chance I would be diagnosed with attention deficit disorder (ADD) today. I couldn't keep my focus on anything for more than five minutes at a time.

I never did super-well in school, but I always managed to get by. When I went to the University of Toronto, I really started to take off and do well. I guess you could say I found my pace there and completed my first year of undergraduate work at the University Of Toronto.

Then my family decided to move to Florida. I applied to and was accepted by the University of Miami. By the way, in case you were wondering, UM wasn't the big party school most people think it was.

I got my undergraduate degree in finance and marketing and am proud to say, I did rather well. I then applied to the master's program at the UM. In contrast to my earlier attention deficit difficulties, I completed the two-year program in one year.

Accomplishing this milestone meant a lot to me and it showed me that I had some real potential. I could be successful in the business world. I realized then, I just had to apply myself a little harder to get what I wanted in life.

I learned from an early age nothing was going to be given to me. Whatever I wanted, I would have to earn on my own. Starting at age 12 until I actually got out of university, I held many different jobs. It wasn't until I started working full-time in the financial services industry that I realized I had found my career.

When I say I had all kinds of jobs, I'm not kidding. I was a professional magician for many, many years and I did about 150 magic shows a year. The Christmas season was the best time of year for me as a magician. A lot of parties wanted entertainment. I took advantage of the demand and built a successful marketing and entertainment business. That taught me many valuable lessons I still use to this very day.

I was also fascinated with airplanes and decided to become a pilot. Golf was another love and although I was never really good at it, I stuck with it and eventually learned to play the game proficiently. In fact, I've actually made two holes-in-one over the years.

I worked in a bike shop, fixing bikes. I was also a cook in a fish store cooking fish and chips. I still have some grease burn marks to prove it. I got them all the way up my arm. Of course, I had a paper route, like most kids.

These jobs were important because they showed me how important it was for me to get an education. If you have children, I implore you to encourage them to work at a young age. Working teaches them invaluable lessons and builds character, confidence and self-reliance.

Some might say it is different today. That it's tougher to get a job, but successful people always find ways to get things done. And as many of my heroes have said in the past, "there's no easy way to do a difficult thing." I can tell you from my own personal experience, that statement is absolutely, 100% true.

Going to the University of Miami had a major impact on my life. It was a great experience. For me, any school would have been a great experience, but I really enjoyed my years at UM. I graduated with honors and when I finished my master's I volunteered to help the alumni association. Eventually, I was elected to the board of directors and eventually served as president of The School of Business Alumni Association.

I ended up teaching at the university for two years as an adjunct professor in the marketing department. I also taught a course every Thursday evening for three hours. That was a long course, but I had a lot of material prepared and it was really enjoyable to teach. In those days, computers were just beginning to become part of the culture. They literally exploded onto the scene. The students liked my course and seemed to get a lot out of it. That was rewarding for me.

Earlier in my life, my father, who was in the insurance business taught me a lot about the business. I learned a lot from him and it taught me the value of mentoring. It ingrained in me a desire to help others learn as well.

Observing my father gave me a good idea of what his professional life was like. I had no idea how to sell insurance, but I saw my father working hard from a very early age. I saw how he got up and went to the office early in the morning and how hard he worked. But he also played hard. I observed how he never confused the two. I saw that he worked hard to earn the ability to play hard. That's me too. I have adopted the same mindset.

I suppose that was the first great lesson I learned as a youngster. Nothing is ever given to you; you have to earn whatever it is you want. As they say, "the world is your oyster—you just have to go out and grab it."

Due to my father's work ethic, our family enjoyed an above-average lifestyle. Frankly, I didn't know any other kind of life, but I figured out that if I wanted those things in my life, the finer things, I was going to have to work for it. To reach my objectives, I knew I had to be honest about how I was going to achieve it; I had to pay the price. It meant I was going to have to go out and do it myself.

Lots of people say they had unhappy childhoods. Not me. I was very fortunate. Observing my father go about his business inspired me. It made me want to be successful and fortunately, I have achieved a significant degree of success.

My mother was a great inspiration as well. She always encouraged me to do well and never give up. She was the glue that kept the family together. She raised four children which was a job in itself.

I can remember my mother taking my father to the airport and saying goodbye to him when I was about 13. He was going to a Million Dollar Round Table meeting. My father exposed me to the

Million Dollar Round Table (MDRT) at a very early age. I knew what it was long before I ever even considered getting into the insurance industry.

For some reason, I recall MDRT was always in June, right around Father's Day. It intrigued me to know the top people in my father's industry were getting together for a meeting.

Once I decided to go into the business, one of my early goals was to qualify for the MDRT. It seemed like back then, July of 1983, the MDRT was just about everyone's goal. To make that happen, I did my first bit of goal setting. I didn't really know it was called goal setting then; but making MDRT was on the top of my mind. I'll tell you more about goal setting later on in the book.

Back then, you qualified for MDRT based on the amount of life insurance you sold. Later, the qualification changed to first-year commissions. The target then was approximately $2.3 million of MDRT credits. Well, my first full year in the business was 1984 and my goal was to qualify for the 1985 MDRT meeting in San Francisco, California. I'll never forget the feeling I had when I qualified for MDRT that year. I made it by December 1984 which qualified me to attend the MDRT annual meeting in San Francisco the following year, 1985. I qualified by doing simple things like having a plan, working it hard, and never giving up.

And speaking of persevering, I've been a member of MDRT every year I've been in the business and I've attended every meeting since 1985.

I know I was provided with a better-than-average lifestyle and with great role models. These helped me get on the right path. I have heard it said so many times, "If it is to be, it is up to me." I was exposed to success at an early age and even though as a child I had no clue what I wanted to do in life, eventually I realized I would be able to do well in what was then called the life insurance business. Today it is referred to as the financial services industry.

How Is Success Defined?

Defining success is an interesting exercise. And the answer can be different for everyone. There are over 300 million people living in the U.S., and each one would define success differently. For the average MDRT member—qualifying for MDRT every year is a minimum personal definition of success—he or she must make approximately 90 to 100 sales per year. That's certainly one way to define success.

Historically, the industry has defined success as 50 sales a year, one sale a week. If you really want to make it in this business, to achieve real success and approach being great, you need to make at least 90 to 100 sales a year.

The average Top of the Table qualification is six times the annual MDRT production requirement. The Top of the Table means you are doing over 300 cases per year, on average. Top of the Table members are averaging almost one sale per day. That's a lot of work, but many people do it. Keep reading and find out how you can do this too. It's hard, but far from impossible. Obviously, there are over 1500 TOT members doing the equivalent every year.

In order to maintain this level of activity, you have to be highly focused, motivated and incredibly well organized. That's what this book is all about—helping you get focused, organized and motivated. So you can move from wherever you are now, to that next level in the near future.

To succeed, you must have a systematic methodology for consistently getting in front of people.

One of the basic rules of change is do NOT dramatically change what you're currently doing, regardless of your current degree of success. If you are a member of the MDRT already, or you're happy with your level of success but you're not yet a member, my advice is keep doing what you're doing, but slowly, incrementally, add an idea or concept to what it is you're already doing and see if it works.

A Little Bit of Wisdom:

It's not the employer who pays the wages. Employers only handle the money. It's the customer who pays the wages.

~ Henry Ford

My First Professional Insurance Experience

When I went to school and graduated in the early 1980s, banking was the big thing. I actually graduated with a finance degree and went out West to look for a job. I wound up in San Diego, went to the university and saw an ad for a job interview. The ad was not specific and it didn't say what kind of job they were interviewing for, but it turned out to be for Mutual of Omaha. The company was recruiting people to join and try to sell insurance.

Well, I was enamored with being out West, more than anything. I had never been on the West Coast and I ended up going on that Mutual of Omaha interview just outside of San Diego. At the interview, they administered a test to determine whether you might be good at sales or not. The test had a score ranging from 0 to 20 and I scored a 13. Good enough to start and they said I'd probably do okay, but they didn't seem to think I'd be able to set the world on fire. So I never took the job. If they didn't show a lot of confidence in me, I didn't want to work for them.

Next, I went to Arizona and I interviewed with a company called American Hospital Supply and they decided not to hire me. I decided to go back to Miami and started looking around at life insurance companies. I must have checked out every insurance company currently doing business in South Florida and soon found myself as an agent with Mass Mutual. I was part of what was called in 1983, the agency system.

I was the type of person whose friends were always doing better than me in school. I said, "I want to prove to me and to my friends that I can do just as well—if not better." That was hard for me to wrap my head around because I was always under the misconception that success meant doing well in school. Mark Twain said, "Never let your schooling interfere with your education." I hadn't heard that quote then, but that was my philosophy too. I instinctively knew I had a lot to learn, and that education was not restricted to the classroom.

The truth is before I graduated from college, or even back when I was in high school, I never thought I would really amount to much.

I said, "You know what, I'm not doing well in school or at least not as well as my friends are doing, so how am I ever going to get a good job and do anything with my life?"

Well, as it turns out, I learned firsthand, that how well you do in school really has no correlation to how well you will do financially in life. The evidence for that is my own result. I do better financially than almost all of my friends today, if you measure success in terms of income. And, importantly, I've had a successful marriage for the past 23 years. I have a wonderful daughter who's 20 years of age. You can say I am living a successful life, so what could be better than that?

When I tell people it's my opinion academic performance is not directly connected to success later in life, they are usually skeptical. Why is there little or no correlation?

I believed you had to do well in school in order to do well financially. I didn't understand that school didn't have any interest in or the tools to measure someone's determination or ability to get things done. Tenacity is the real ingredient to long-term success. Nothing measures that like doing the work. Schools can't measure a person's character or patience or capacity for perseverance. There's no test anywhere that can do this. And those are the real, tangible qualities that determine success, not getting a high grade on a math exam or a science test or a social studies thesis.

I attribute my success to my ability to focus and get things done—I have a gift for doing the job right. And that's probably where I shine over and above many other people. And the beautiful thing about it is you can actually learn how to focus and get things done. For every one person born with an innate ability to concentrate on the task at hand, I'd guess there are ten who had to learn how to do it.

Communication is key in sales. As the expression goes, "No one cares how much you know until they know how much you care." And if you can't communicate how much you care about your prospects, they'll never become your clients.

This is one of the gifts I have, my ability to communicate with people and to get them to trust me and take action on my recommendations. Communication is the hallmark of all successful sales professionals.

I believe selling is not just for those who have the innate ability to communicate. In addition, you must also be born with a burning desire to achieve. But again, if not, you can acquire this talent. The difference between success and failure is so slight. It is usually determined by someone's willingness to pay the price to become successful. Paying the price means a lot of things, including the willingness to delay gratification, to put in the hours required for you to meet your goals, and then focusing on the details others would rather not deal with.

Look at Tiger Woods (forget about the scandal). Yes, he was born with natural ability and talent; but that does not mean the guy did not need the world's best coaches, or that he did not need to work harder than most every other golfer in the world to get what he wants. Without work, talent curls up and dies. It requires effort. You cannot be successful and lazy.

Look, too, at Michael Jordan. Did he possess great skills? Absolutely! Was he the first one to practice and the last to leave? Yes, he was. So the point I'm trying to make is the difference between success and failure is dedication and hard, focused work. Here is the great paradox. The easy way almost always turns out to be the hard way. Why? Because it doesn't work and you've wasted your time and you are still back at square one.

I remember a boy who I went to high school with. He was a smart kid, but refused to "waste" time studying. Instead, he constructed these elaborate ways to cheat on tests. Some of the ways were ingenious, like writing answers in pen on his wrist, or writing answers in tiny letters on a piece of paper and then rolling that paper up and inserting it into the barrel of a ballpoint pen.

One day I said to him, "If you would spend just half the time studying as you do in figuring out methods to cheat, you'd be much better off and benefit from your effort." He never paid any attention to me, and today he's not very successful. Very smart academically, yes. Very successful financially, no. And with his mind, he could have been a very rich person, but he wanted the easy way, and it turned out to be the hard way.

One of the other things about my background is I always wanted to do a lot of different things from a very young age. My parents never discouraged me from doing any of them.

I mentioned before that as a teenager, I was a magician. I was doing magic shows for churches, synagogues, birthday parties, family events, et cetera, and sometimes I would have audiences of 100 or 150 people at a time.

When I was 18 and doing the shows, it taught me how to perform in front of people. That's important because in my company—Silverman Financial—one of our fundamental sales strategies is to do a lot of workshops. The skills I use today I acquired at a younger age—and all that work and experience paid off for me later in life. But at the time, I had no comprehension of how much it would really help me.

Another thing that's essential is to understand the value of looking back at your life and thinking about those hobbies and interests you had as a kid and seeing if there is anything about them you can use and integrate into what you're doing in your business today. What interested you as a kid could give you some good clues as to skills and abilities you have as assets for today. In my case, performing magic before large audiences gave me a great deal of poise and confidence when "performing" at a workshop filled with prospective and existing clients.

A lot of people, unfortunately, overlook their inherent skills and don't realize how some of what they did in the past might help them today.

My father taught me something at a young age. It still rings true forty years later and it always will. He said to me, "No matter what you do in life if you do it to the best of your ability, if you're honest with people, if you're the best at whatever it is you do, you are always going to do well financially."

Even if you're a trash collector, be the very best trash collector there is. If you are, you will do well financially.

I never forgot his words. And although there are people who have vastly larger incomes than I do, it doesn't bother me because I'm doing the best that I, Marc Silverman can do—and that turns out to be pretty good, indeed.

Another thing I hope you keep in mind is that you should not try to be me, Marc Silverman. Don't try to be Sid Friedman, don't try to be Marv Feldman and don't try to be Tony Gordon or Guy Baker. Just be the best you that you can be and you will be shocked at how you will prosper.

I hope you will continue to read this book, take ideas from it and weave them into your own approach to conduct your professional life.

Just because one idea works for me doesn't mean it's necessarily going to work for you, but there are an infinite number of ideas out there that will help you grow personally and professionally. To find them, all you need to do is to look.

Why a Book?

Let me elaborate on why I am writing this book.

I have been fortunate and blessed to be asked to speak all over the world. I've spoken in China, New Zealand, Australia, Shanghai, Taipei, Israel, Dubai, the United Kingdom, all over the United States and Canada. I've given talks in Singapore. And everywhere I go, I'm asked by agents to put something in writing because they would like to study what I have taught and they believe they could really learn a lot from a book based on my ideas, techniques and strategies.

The primary purpose of writing this book is to help agents discover skills and techniques that can get them to the next level. It's often been said if you are successful, you have a responsibility to give something back and share.

I am not writing this book to make a fortune because I can certainly make more money working with my clients then I could ever earn marketing a book. However, since I believe part of my duty is to give back to the industry, I believe documenting what has helped me achieve sales success will help you and other agents. If you aspire to higher levels of production, there are ideas in this book that can get you to wherever you want to go.

One of the things I hope will happen is that agents will learn from my mistakes. I have heard it said that a fool learns from his own mistakes, but a wise person learns from the mistakes of others. If that is true, then you have a tremendous opportunity to learn from me. I have made many mistakes over the years. This book should enable you to get to the next level a lot less painfully.

Keep in mind this book is not about how to sell. I want you to know what makes Marc Silverman tick. You can read and learn how I have disciplined myself to achieve at high sales levels. Hopefully you will find some of my techniques valuable and you can easily customize it to fit your own circumstances.

Discipline is a main ingredient to become successful. I learned early in my career that discipline involves doing the things you must do that unsuccessful people are unwilling to do.

It is true. There is a price to pay for success. If you are willing to pay the price, you will reach your goals. If you are not, then you are likely to never grow beyond where you are today.

To understand where I am today, it is important you understand what it was like for me when I started. I laid the foundation then for what I do today. I think this will give you some idea of the price I paid to get started. It will give you ideas on how I set goals, how I wrote down my goals year by year and how I established a plan to achieve those goals.

I also want you to understand how my involvement in the Million Dollar Round Table helped me grow and become who I am today. I am going to share with you what I learned about prospecting. Most importantly, I want to give you many ideas you can employ tomorrow morning without spending a lot of money. If you do what I did, you will be able to see the people that you need to see to make your sales goals.

So let's get started.

1

Starting Out

I mentioned I started right out of university working for Mass Mutual. One of the things I didn't tell you was I actually sold door to door as a youngster. I sold theater tickets for a very large theater company in Toronto. I remember getting the job and I had no idea how to sell. I went to meet with the manager in downtown Toronto. He told me my goal was to sell theater tickets. I would be paid so much for each ticket I sold.

So I said, "Well, how do I do that?" He said, "You've got to go door to door, just knock on the doors." That probably wouldn't work very well today, not many people will open a door for a stranger—but this was back in 1974.

The manager said to me, "Selling is a numbers game. You're going to get a lot of noes, but the more noes you get the more yeses you will get." He told me, "I have a friend called 'See-More Sell-More.' The more people you see, the more people you're going to sell."

I was really new and inexperienced at that time. I didn't completely understand all he meant by this, but I learned a lesson way back then that still applies today. I learned he was right. The more doors I knocked on, the better I did. And he was correct when he said I would get a lot of noes but I also got a few yeses every week.

I didn't keep that job very long because I didn't really like walking door to door, but the lesson I learned has been paid forward. Agents today should not be satisfied making one or two sales a week. Fifty to 100 sales a year is a good job. But if you want to reach high levels of sales success, I believe you must see as many people during the week as possible because you're going to get a lot of noes, but you're also going to get a lot of yeses.

For example, in my office there are two sales people who see approximately 25 people each week. Add that up. It is about 1200 prospects a year. We sell to about 350 of these people every year. In other words, we close about one out of three prospects. I am satisfied with this ratio. It is the result of a lot of years of learning and a lot a years of hard work. But it is achievable if you just make it your goal, establish a plan and stick to your plan.

Can you imagine if I was only seeing 100 people a year? If that were the case, I'd have to close most of them or turn them into really large cases in order to make a living. Now, I don't mind if I lose one or two sales or ten sales because when you're making 350 sales a year, in the long run, losing ten of them isn't going to really matter. This is truly the Law of LARGE Numbers.

Suppose, however, you are making only 50 sales a year and you lose ten of them. That's 20% of your production, right there. That's quite a bit of leakage. I don't recommend that anyone put themselves in that position. See a lot of people and get a lot of yeses. Focus on the prospects and the sales will take care of themselves. This assumes of course, you know the basics of selling.

2

Keeping In Touch

When you hear the word no—don't be discouraged. No can mean a lot of different things. Usually it is the starting point. I can't tell you the number of sales I have made simply by following up and getting back to people who told me "no."

For example, I have a habit of calling everyone on their birthday—at least I try to. I recently made two large sales in the same month by calling people I hadn't spoken to in several years. I just called and wished them a happy birthday. I actually reached them when I called and one thing led to another. Before you knew it, I was into a sales presentation and they ended up doing business with me.

That extra little effort paid off, and there are plenty of other things you can do in addition to making happy birthday calls.

I was told by a successful role model that the key to success is to work half a day, every day and it doesn't matter which 12 hours. I'm no stranger to 12-hour-long days. I'm also no stranger to playing hard for 12 hours, either. If you want to work hard for 12 hours and play hard for 12 hours, just make sure they're not the same 12 hours!

Most people want success but are not willing to pay the price. There is no easy way to do a difficult thing. Are you willing to make a sacrifice to accomplish what you want?

3

Review Old Calendar Books

Do you keep all of your old calendar books? I hope so. I do. I keep them in a safe place. They are valuable to me. Here's why:

I have saved my old calendar books from all the years gone by. I have every book since I have ever been in the business. And if I find times are a little bit slow, (that rarely happens anymore), I will sit down with a glass of wine, pull out my calendar book from a few years ago and go through it. I ask myself, "Who didn't buy from me? Who haven't I seen in a while? Who do I need to call whom I haven't been in touch with for a couple of years?" And before you know it, I have a list of 30 or 40 people to call. I will start to call this list until I start getting busy again. And sometimes, just those calls will start generating sales for me. I will get busy again, just from reviewing my old calendar books.

When you save appointment books for 27 years, there are a lot of names in the books you might tend to overlook. In a sense, it's like found money. And I never worry about people I can't find or people who don't want to talk to me. Those are the noes I need to get to the yeses.

4

No Doesn't Necessarily Mean No

As you have probably figured out, a no right now doesn't mean no forever. I saw a client recently who was going to invest $100,000 with me. I sent him an e-mail, I followed up, I did everything I was supposed to do, but I never heard back from him.

I let it go for several weeks. I just didn't bother him. Then I called him again. He said to me, "You know, Marc, I've just been so busy. I'm glad you called." I told him I was going to be in my Broward office that day. He said, "Can we get together later?"

The result, later that day he came in and I picked up another $100,000 just because I was persistent.

Remember this: "Persistence wears down resistance."

I think starting out with Mass Mutual in an agency system was probably the best place for me to begin my career. I got my feet wet and learned in a system that held me accountable. At the risk of offending anyone, that is not my intention, I believe most super-successful agents ultimately move out of an agency system. Today, they are out on their own.

The agency system was a great place for me to cut my teeth and I learned a lot. But eventually, if you are really going to develop yourself professionally, you will want to have your own identity and organization. It is expensive and will require you to manage your organization. But it will give you independence and the sense you are in business for yourself. You also need to be involved in a study group and be part of the Million Dollar Round Table. In addition, there are other professional organizations such as AALU, CLU, SFSP and your local chapters of NAIFA. To keep learning, it is important to be involved in a study group. My study group has been integral to my personal development. I have been attending for the last 23 years. Form one with other agents you meet who are like-minded and want a support group. It is a great way to learn and have some fun at the same time.

5

Why Stay Involved In Study Groups?

What causes me to stay involved in a study group and MDRT is that I'm always learning. When you stop learning you wither up and die intellectually. When you're green, you grow and when you're ripe you rot. I don't want to rot. I want to grow and keep on learning and studying and maintaining an open mind. This helps keep me green. The same is true of prospecting. When you stop prospecting you die as well. So, you must keep learning and you learn by being involved with people who are doing as well as you are doing or even better. There is always someone who has something valuable to share with you.

You can learn from others, no matter whom it is or what they are doing. I have discovered and totally believe if you become involved and regularly attend a study group or industry meetings, you will learn. Let me give you a warning, you can get over-involved. What I mean is, you can belong to too many groups, go to too many industry meetings, belong to too many community organizations, like the Chamber of Commerce, et cetera. I pick my spots and limit what I do because I just don't have the time to be involved in all of those things. So I limit myself to the activities that yield the most benefit.

A Little Bit of Wisdom:

Let your hook be always cast; in the pool where you least expect it, there will be a fish.

~ Ovid

6

Pick a Specialty and Do It Well

When I first started, I picked out one product, disability insurance, and concentrated on becoming an expert in the contractual features and benefits. For anyone who is new to the business, I would recommend doing the same thing. Identify your niche and do one thing really well rather than try to be a jack of all trades and master of none. Of course, you need to know all the planning basics, but then you will ultimately find a niche market, something you really like. When you find something you really like, specialize in it. After all, if you needed surgery, would you go to a generalist or a specialist?

Suppose you have just started in the business. And suppose you are in an agency where they teach you about life insurance, disability insurance, pension planning, term insurance, whole life insurance, universal life insurance, split dollar, annuities, and buy/sell agreements. It is important to learn all you can about each of these concepts and products. But you then need to position yourself to specialize in one area.

When I first started out, my area of specialization was disability income protection. What I did was call on attorneys. I got hold of the Dade County Bar Association book. It had about 6000 attorneys listed and I called about 15 each and every week. Attorneys are usually successful financially. I wanted to call on people with money.

I did that for 10-plus years and I probably sold 300 policies. I was an expert in this area and attorneys knew I specialized in disability. As a result, I started getting referrals to other attorneys who wanted someone who really knew the subject. It was a great way to get started and it helped me expand my markets and develop a comfort level with another profession, CPAs.

You can do the same thing with CPAs, doctors, specialties within the medical community and other associations like veterinarians and business owners. You name it, they probably have an association. Become a specialist and become known for your knowledge and expertise.

7

Getting Out of Life Insurance

Years ago, I wanted to get off the life insurance treadmill because it was obvious there was going to be no major residual income from the sale of life insurance in the future. Renewals were going away. If you are going to build a business, you must have retention income. Retention income is income that will be there year after year. I wanted to get into the money management field.

For years, I noticed every January that my renewal commissions were declining and it was getting harder and harder to write new life insurance business. I didn't want to continue working that hard so I could keep pace with my prior year's income. I wanted to know I would have a good strong money flow whether I worked or I didn't. It is the same concept as renewal commissions only the trails from money under management are much more reliable and steady.

When I realized how much my renewal commissions were declining, it caused me to reassess my business model. I did that approximately 11 years ago. That was when I decided to start asking prospects if we could help them manage their retirement assets. Another real advantage to building a money management practice is you have something to sell when the time comes. There are companies which will buy your stream of income from money management for usually a two times multiple. It is a cash cow for them and adds to their bottom line with no prospecting.

Agents who only sell life insurance really don't have a business they can sell to someone else. It is almost impossible to transfer prospective names of future sales to a serious buyer for fair market value. In the life insurance business, you are only as good as your last sale.

8

Target Marketing

I heard a speaker once tell me, years ago, you really need to be target marketing rather than trying to be all things to all people. And when I became a specialist rather than a generalist, my income started to soar.

As a result, I specialized. It was hard to give up my old ways, but I knew I had to do it if I was going to reach my goals. If you were to ask what it is I do, I would tell you my firm focuses on working with people who are retired or getting ready to retire. We help them make the transition into retirement seamlessly. We help them feel happy and confident about their financial future and feel they are being taken care of and serviced properly. That's our value proposition. It is what we offer clients who are considering using our firm for their financial management. They are buying financial freedom.

We don't provide other services. We don't try to be all things to all people. I discovered you must "Target your market," so you can reach a large number of people who are in the same affinity group. As your reputation grows, your income will grow dramatically. I did this when I first started in the business and now I am still doing it, only in a different way. I continue to do it for one basic reason—it works! I always know when an idea works for an agent because they stop using the idea.

A Little Bit of Wisdom:

Losers make promises they often break. Winners make commitments they always keep.

~ Denis Waitley

9

Know Your Product and Know It Well

If you really want to become successful and make a difference in your community you must learn to stand out in the crowd. You must build a reputation in your target market and you really need to know your stuff. It makes all the difference in the financial world. Prospects are looking for help. They want leaders and they want to know they have the best advisor helping them with their financial needs. Selling is 98% people knowledge and 2% product knowledge—but in order to succeed, you better know 100% of that 2%.

In other words, know your product incredibly well, but know people even better. That's essential to being successful in the financial services business.

> **A Little Bit of Wisdom:**
> **Luck is what happens when preparation meets opportunity.**
> ~ Coach Darrel Royal

10

Not Everyone's Yes Means the Same Thing

I told you earlier, everyone's no is the same—people are saying they are just not interested and, at least for now, you have no sale. But everyone's yes isn't the same. What do I mean by this? Simply, someone who is making $200,000/year and says "yes" is quite a bit different than someone who is making $50,000 a year.

The $200,000 prospect's yes means a lot more to you than the $50,000 prospect's yes. So make sure you are asking the right people for money. This is a hard lesson to learn, but it is worth it. For approximately the same amount of effort you will expend calling on people with medium to low incomes, you can call on wealthy prospects and wind up earning significantly more in fees and commissions. All noes are the same, regardless of income. But a wealthy prospect's yes means more than a less wealthy prospect's yes. So if you're going to start prospecting with enthusiasm, start calling on people who have money and can write big checks.

When I first started calling on attorneys, I picked up all the disability contracts I could find from all the major carriers and started reading them. I wanted to learn their features and benefits. If I was going to be an expert, I needed to know all the ins and outs of the contracts. I had to train myself to be an expert even though I did not fully realize what I was doing. You know what I mean, "Fake it until you make it." I asked a lot of questions. I called the experts in the home office to discuss their disability contracts and the technical subtleties of each benefit. They were great resources. The more I learned, the more I knew disability was going to be my specialty. Remember, knowledge is power.

A Little Bit of Wisdom:

When I discovered a reluctant prospect, I would say: "Hey Charlie, if you get sick or injured, I can send you either a check or a get-well card, which would you prefer?"

Sometimes I would ask them, "If you were going to a doctor for a particular problem, would you rather go to a specialist or a generalist?" Most prospects always say a specialist. I tell them, "Well, I am a specialist. This is all I do. I will give you the best advice you are going to get. No one knows these products like I do."

Newer agents starting out should become a specialist in something. They need to focus on one, specific area. It doesn't matter what it is. It can be financial planning or pensions or something else. But learn everything you can about it and then run with it rather than try to be all things to all people. The agency system wants agents to be generalists. This gives you a wider market. But over the long haul, based on my experience, I am convinced you will do much better by specializing. Be known by the problems you solve, not the solutions you sell.

There are only two types of sales: the easy ones and the ones you don't get.

In one sense, all sales are easy. If you are with someone who says to you, "Look, all I really want is $500,000 of term," don't argue. Pull out an application and get them to sign it. Make them a client, and then you can work on converting the term later. One of the worst things anyone can do is instead of being quiet and writing up the application, you keep talking and talking. Don't ever make the mistake of talking yourself out of a sale. The worst thing you can do is to have the prospect wind up saying, "Never mind."

Remember, there are only two sales, the easy ones and the ones you don't get. All sales seem easy—if you make them.

11

Making Phone Calls

I want to tell you a little bit about how I used the telephone to generate business. This is exactly how I did it.

Here is my strategy. In the beginning I would make all the phone calls for appointments and for meetings. I would start the year off by setting my goal at 200 lives. If you are new, that may sound like a lot, but if you break it down monthly it's only 17 a month or about 4 per week. If you are going to be in the business, you may as well be in it.

Then I worked backwards. First, I figured out how many people I actually needed to see in order to make those sales. I kept accurate count of all my phone calls, how many people I saw in a given month and how many sales I made. I had to know my numbers. If I knew my numbers, I would then know my percentages and then I knew exactly how many weeks I had left in the year to accomplish my goals.

Based on my percentages, I knew I had to see 454 people in order to make 200 sales because my closing ratio was 44%. So I knew I had to see 38 people every month to close 17 cases. By extrapolation, I needed to see about 10 prospects per week. I knew if I did this consistently, I would make my goals.

I had to build in margin. I knew I had to make almost double my appointments to make my target number of sales. This was because 50% of the people in my very early years would cancel on me. While that was discouraging, it also was a statistic I could count on. In other words, if I had 15 meetings set up in a given week I would actually only hold 7 or 8 appointments. It was a fact of life, people would invariably cancel. So I had to plan for it.

As I gained more and more experience, I was able to qualify my prospects more effectively over the phone. In other words, I wouldn't set the appointment up if I sensed they were going to cancel. As a result, I had fewer and fewer cancellations. This meant I was able to work more efficiently.

I don't mean to say I was able to eliminate cancellations. I would still get some, but I would also make new appointments during the week. That way, my cancellation ratio was almost zero.

When I started the week with 20 meetings, I might see 15 people who made appointments the previous week. Invariably we made five or six new meetings during the week so in essence, I really had zero cancellations.

Now I hold just about all of my appointments in my office. If a prospective client agrees to come to my office, they are much less likely to cancel. Why? Because they had to be serious in the first place when they made the appointment or they would never have agreed to come to my office. On the other hand, if someone makes an appointment to have you come to their home or office, it doesn't take much of a commitment on their part. They can say, "Sure, come on over." But when I get there, they may be too busy or just not answer the door. When they agree to visit your office, it means they truly consider the appointment important and they want to hear what you have to offer. Remember, the home team always has the advantage. You know how you get people to come to your office? You ask them. It will work if you ask them. How many of you reading this have a doctor come to your home?

12

Tracking Your Numbers

Every year, I set my income goals for the next 52 weeks. I break them down into manageable segments. One of the things I recommend is for you to start tracking your numbers. How many calls do you make in a given week? How many people do you actually get through to? How many people who talk to you ultimately grant you an appointment?

So you'll know if you make 100 calls in a week you are going to get to speak to 12 people and six will grant you an interview. This is great information to know. And remember, this happens even though I fail to reach 88% of those on my call list. If I close half of the appointments I see, I feel I am getting excellent results!

You must know your ratios. It is the only way you can build a business plan and have any confidence you are going to hit your goals. If you knew right now that for every 100 calls you made you would yield six appointments and three sales, how many times would you do this? And if those three sales earned you $15,000 in commission, that would mean for every call you made whether someone answered the phone or not, you would earn on average $150 in income. If you knew that was true, how many times a day would you pick up your phone? Plenty, I would bet! To learn more go to page 172.

A Little Bit of Wisdom:

You don't get paid for the hour. You get paid for the value you bring to the hour.

~ Jim Rohn

13

Keeping Records

If someone is struggling, I always know the reason. They are not keeping records. Keeping records is so important.

Someone did a thirty-year study of the Harvard class of 1959. This was done after the class graduated. The study showed 10% of those people were very adamant about keeping records of their activities. The study discovered that the record-keepers had a higher net worth than the other 90% put together. What does that tell you? It tells me there are huge benefits from being able to review what you've done. To know your ratios is to be able to predict your results. It means you can find out how to do things better and you can also—as in the case of my reviewing past calendar books—find contacts and leads you have forgotten or failed to call for several years.

A Little Bit of Wisdom:

You have to do what others won't, to achieve what others don't.

~ Anonymous

14

What Kinds of Records are Important?

Remember this: all records serve some purpose. Whether it's to help cut expenses or increase income, well-kept records are your best resource for determining the best way to improve. The number of phone calls you make, how many people you're contacting and the number of appointments you make are all data you can use to increase your bottom line. But if you don't have the records, you are missing a big opportunity. And to succeed in this business, you can't afford to miss a single chance to cut costs or increase income.

Granted this is all very simple stuff, but that does not mean people do it. As a matter of fact, most people do not do it. Remember the Harvard study. Record-keepers tend to prosper while non-record keepers tend to not succeed at a high level.

I have a set time I make my calls every day. By knowing your numbers and getting yourself organized to make your phone calls from 9:00 to 10:30 every day, for example, and by having your appointments come in to your office at predetermined times according to your own schedule, you are managing your time effectively. You are fitting people into your schedule rather than just going with whatever comes your way.

You have to decide when you want to see appointments. Maybe when you are just starting out your career, you should see people at their convenience, but once you develop a steady flow of prospects, you have to begin to control your schedule. You'd be surprised to see how many prospects will respect you even more if they realize you are a professional. That you are very busy and that your time is very valuable. No one puts more value on your time than you will. Lots of sales success is based on how the prospects perceive you. Tell them something like, "I can see you here at either 1:30PM on Tuesday, or 11:00AM on Wednesday," so they will get the message and the impression you are a serious professional. They will be a lot less likely to waste their time—and yours.

15

Stay Disciplined

When I first started out in this industry, I disciplined myself to spend every morning from 9:00AM until 10:30AM making my phone calls for appointments.

I guarded this time jealously and wouldn't let anyone or anything disturb me. No one could come into my office. I wouldn't let anyone upset my rhythm. I didn't care who was calling me back or what they wanted, I disciplined myself to make the calls and stay on track from 9:00AM until 10:30AM.

There is a reason I did my calling at this hour. I live in a big city and the traffic is horrendous early in the morning. I didn't want to be driving to some appointment early in the morning just to find myself sitting in traffic. So I figured I'd make my phone calls during this time instead of wasting time driving.

Early in my career, my goal was to have my first appointment set at 11:00AM and then have another one at 1:00PM. My next slot was at 2:30PM and then I would have my last appointment at 4:00PM. I then would head back to my office, dictating notes, filling out paperwork for the day and getting ready for the next day. I soon discovered that when most agents were leaving for home, I was just getting back to my office to fill out paperwork. This discipline drove my success. I have heard it said, "that what you do from 9AM to 5PM pays your bills and gives you a decent income, but what you do before 9AM and after 5PM is what makes you rich." That is exactly how it has worked out for me. As I said earlier, there is no substitute for hard work.

16

Goal Setting

Early in life, I was a stickler for goal setting. I don't know whether this was taught to me or how I learned the habit. Maybe I just learned it on my own. But I said, "You know what, I've got to be disciplined to run my business as a business, otherwise, I will fail."

I learned through observation that most sales people—and most people in general—go to work, but that's it. They have an employee mentality. They think that showing up is half the game, but I don't believe this is true. Showing up just gets you into the game, but you have to work very hard to win the game. Most people get to the stadium, but they don't have a financial game plan in order to win. Goals tell you where you want to go; recordkeeping tells you if you are going to get there.

You have got to have a plan. You have to know how to achieve your goal. I think you need to carefully set your goals in order to be successful. If you are just out there selling and not setting a goal, why are you doing it? Stephen Covey says, "Start with the end in mind." What is the end game? Why are you working? Why are you doing what you're doing? You need to be shooting for something specific. Have you heard it said, "If you aim for the stars and miss, you can still hit the moon"? Hitting the moon is a pretty good result in most cases. Don't be afraid to set a big goal and go for it. The only thing you have to lose is mediocrity. to learn more see pages 175 and 178.

17

Three Levels of Income Goal Setting: Conservative, Realistic and Aggressive

An important element of goal setting involves what I think of as guaranteed income. This comes from your renewal commissions. This is the commission that flows into your business every month, every year. It is the income your business generates even if you bring in no new business.

I decided to calculate how much revenue my practice would receive before I even get out of bed every January 1. Theoretically, an agent who runs a business with the same volume I do could easily earn over seven figures annually before he or she writes the first piece of business that year.

I created three levels of anticipated annual revenue as part of my goal-setting activities. I start with a conservative goal, a realistic goal and an aggressive goal. And I always try to target my sales activities so I achieve my aggressive goal. Remember the stars and the moon?

I add to my aggressive goal the amount of money I need to earn annually to cover the basics and necessities we enjoy as a family. The basic costs include things like my life insurance premiums, social security contributions, what my office overhead will cost me in a given year, my projected income taxes and my retirement plan contributions, as well as miscellaneous business expenses.

And I figure out exactly what I need monthly and compare this figure to what I am bringing in monthly. The difference is what I need to earn in order to juggle all the balls I have in the air and keep them under control.

In addition, I also set my investment and saving goals. It is an important part of goal setting to keep your own personal financial situation in order. As a financial advisor, you don't want to be worried about your own financial well-being when you counsel others. You do this by not having credit card debt, which you accomplish by keeping a lot of money in the bank and paying cash for all of your purchases. Try to get as many of your bills paid as you can. An easier solution is don't spend a lot of money.

Right now, as I am writing this book, my house is paid for and my cars are paid for. I have a lot of cash in the bank and I have a lot of life insurance and disability insurance. I owe nothing on credit card debt. I accomplished this by setting my goals and achieving them. Paying these items off is a function of the discipline I have built into my system. How are you disciplined?

You are a financial teacher. If you are going to teach people how to act financially responsible, then isn't it reasonable that you must do this yourself? I can't tell you how many sales I've made by showing people my financial statements and where I invest my money. I show them the products I own myself.

I remember one client who was a good friend. He asked me, "Do you own this yourself?" I was a little taken aback by his boldness, but I thought, you know what, he has every right to know. So I showed him my personal portfolio of insurance. He said, "Marc, if you own it, that's good enough for me. I'm going to buy it." I did own it and I do own a lot of the products I recommend to my clients.

This is a strong and powerful statement. It shows your clients you are walking your talk. Show people your own financial net worth statement, if you have a pretty good net worth. Show them where you keep your money and how you invest. This has worked very successfully for me through the years.

I want to reiterate this important message. Sales people need to get their own financial house in order before they can hope to really help other people do it. To learn more go to page 177.

18

The One Card System

When I first started in this industry, I learned a personal business organization system called The O. Alfred Granum—One Card System. This was a prospecting method I used long before computers became ubiquitous.

I think The One Card System is just as relevant today and still as prevalent as it was then. The system was simple. Every time I got a referral, I wrote the prospect's name down on a 3X5 card and put it in my prospect stack. It forced me to follow up. I assigned points to all my activities. I got points for closing a sale, opening a sale, making a sales presentation and getting a referral.

The idea was to earn so many points per week. I started doing this right when I started because I had no other methodology to really keep track of my activity. It made me work and it really did work.

Today, I don't use the One Card System any longer. We do it completely different in my office today—with computers and databases, but as a new, young agent just starting out, it worked well for me.

A Little Bit of Wisdom:
Having once decided to achieve a certain task, achieve it at all costs of tedium and distaste. The gain in self-confidence of having accomplished a tiresome labor is immense.
~ Thomas A. Bennett

19

Never Give Up

Winston Churchill gave many speeches. In one of his more memorable speeches he stood before a large crowd of graduating students and he said these words, "Never ever, ever, ever, ever, ever, ever give up." Then he turned around and left, so the story goes. Winston Churchill's determination to never quit saved England during World War II. That same determination kept me going in the financial services business until I had confidence I could not only survive, but I could thrive.

I promise you, you will be beaten down. You will be chopped down. You will have many people tell you no in many different ways. You will have many doors closed in your face. But the key to success is to be disciplined and to never ever, ever give up.

If your goal is alive and worthwhile, you've got to stay the course and be true to your goals, work your plan—because ultimately, your plan will work.

Consider all of the Las Vegas casinos. They make a lot of money and they know that any given night they will win a lot of money. They also know they can lose a lot of money, but in the long run, they have the percentages on their side. They know they are always going to make money. They know the odds and they know the odds are always stacked in their favor.

It is the same in our business. We have the odds stacked in our favor as well. To achieve financial success, we just have to do the small things every single day and do them to the best of our ability. If you do, you will become successful.

Remember, it's the little things you do today that will ultimately determine your success down the road. It's the everyday chopping of the wood, swinging the bat, doing the things you must do that ordinary people won't do, that will make you become super successful.

I remember when I took the Certified Financial Planner's exam. I had to take it three times before I ultimately passed it. Most people would have given up because of their inability to tolerate failure. But I wanted that designation. It was my goal, but it was an onerous task to pass the exam and it took years of study. I never missed by much either time I failed. And I know a lot of people who have failed the exam and have not gone back and tried again. It was too demanding for them and they didn't want to pay the price.

Never ever give up. Stick with your goals. It is the difference between setting a goal and actually achieving it. Failure is not fatal, quitting is.

A Little Bit of Wisdom:

He that is good for making excuses is seldom good for anything else.

~ Benjamin Franklin

20

Personal and Professional Goals

It is important to have other goals besides financial goals. I think you should also have personal goals. For example; you might have spiritual goals and goals for personal development. You might have physical fitness goals or goals related to how much time you want to spend with your children, your spouse, and your elderly parents. Whatever is important to you should be converted into a written objective. Why? If keeps you focused and holds you accountable. Anyone can dream. But dreaming with purpose will bring you great success. Dream in color.

Some of my professional goals were to become a CLU, a CHFC and a CFP. I accomplished those goals. Again, I wasn't the greatest student and I had to read things two or three times to really digest the information. But the difference was, I would read it two or three times to get it done—and I did get it done.

Those are the little things that can help you make big changes.

21

The Month of December

There's another element to goal setting I call The Month of December. Every month I write in my records the results I have achieved. I do this daily. I keep track of the date of sale. I track whether this is a new sale or a repeat sale. If it is a new client, I record the client's full name, the amount of the premium, the commission we will earn, the type of sale I made, the insurance company and any other relevant information.

Let me make up some numbers to help explain how this works and why it is important. Let's say, for example, in December of 2008, I wrote down the total number of cases sold for the year—298. Total commissions were a little over $2.2 million and total premiums were a little over $39 million for the year.

I know these sound like big numbers at first. But when you break them down to monthly production, it's not really all that big. A total of 298 means I did 25 sales a month. That is only 5 to 6 a week or one a day. My average commission per sale was about $7500 per case. If it was all annuities and the average commission rate is 5%, then my average sale was $130,000.

The important key to goal setting is breaking down your goals weekly, even daily. It you are going to achicvc your overall game plan, you have to have a step by step process to get you to the end of the game. The point is that you must develop your own numbers. My numbers are important to me and make sense to me. You must do it in a way that makes sense to you. To learn more go to page 170.

A Little Bit of Wisdom:

Success isn't a result of spontaneous combustion. You must set yourself on fire.

~ ***Arnold H. Glasgow***

22

Get a Mentor

Get a Coach—The trend today is for professional athletes to get a coach, to find someone who will hold them accountable and push them to their potential.

You can do the same thing in this business. If you really want to grow, you may want to find a mentor. If you look at all the great athletes today, they're still working with coaches even though they are the best athletes in the world. Why do they have a coach? Because a coach can see things the athlete will miss and they can point out subtle changes that will make all the difference.

As an example, I decided I needed a coach. So I visited with a strategic coach in Canada for three years. They helped me achieve better success and clarity in goal setting and helped me figure out how to get to the next level of income and production.

I said earlier that I thought joining the MDRT—the Million Dollar Round Table, was one of the most important decisions I made in my career. You might want to know how you can achieve Million Dollar Round Table status. First, you need to find out the production requirements necessary to qualify for the Million Dollar Round Table.

Let us assume the minimum first-year commission requirements for membership in 2010 is $100,000 of new first-year commissions.

Assume further, this is important enough for you to make it a priority during the year. First, break down the annual goal into a monthly objective. That would be only $8300 a month. Then, break it down further into a weekly goal for 52 weeks. That's $1923 a week. If you are averaging three sales a week, that's $641 per sale, that's not all that much. When you look at it that way, making MDRT is not so overwhelming. It is within reach.

There is an old expression. It starts with a question, "How do you eat an elephant?" An elephant is a big animal but you can do it, "One bite at a time." In other words, if you break down your objective into little steps, each step does not look so unattainable. It is the mountain that looks formidable.

Speaking of elephants, remember that the gestation period for an elephant is five years. Most big things don't happen quickly. You've got to be patient and give yourself the time needed to get to where you ultimately want to be. The worst thing you can do is create unreasonable expectations and then feel like a failure because you didn't achieve your goal. Start with reasonable expectations and then increase them as you gain momentum.

23

Sales Results Book

I told you about "The Month of December." This is when I start to tally up my results for the year. This is when I transfer my records into my sales results book each year. Going back to 1983, for each year I've been in business, I have a book I can pull off my shelf that shows me all of my records for that year. Each book is not identical because I have made some changes to the process over the years, Currently there are now sections in the book that cover my investment results, my pension plan contributions and values, all my expenses, my updated financial statements, my goal setting, my income flow and my top client profile.

One of the things you can do with a sales results book is see how much growth you have achieved over the years. You can look at whether you are making progress. It is a tool to help you analyze your top 20%. Where is most of your income being derived? From which clients, how did you get to them, what was the purpose of the sale? These are important questions you need to know if you are running a business.

I have shared this idea with some of my clients because I think it is important for them to see how I organize my life. It gives them a sense that they can have confidence in me and it makes them feel pretty good about me because they can see I am watching the details. It is not hard for them to extrapolate that if I do this for me, I am doing it for them, that I'm able to take care of them just as well.

24

Track Your Calls

Another detail that is important—I also used to track the calls I made in a week. I would keep count of the appointments I set and the number of appointments I actually held. I would track the appointments made to start each week, the appointments kept, new prospects, and the written first-year commissions. Then I would track all of that monthly and adjust my activities for the upcoming months. Most people don't take the time to track their calls, and they are missing a great opportunity to generate more appointments, which always develops into more business, which means more commission.

It is important that you know your metrics. This is how you can determine whether you are making progress and where you need to improve. Goal setting and accountability are two important ingredients to long-term success.

A Little Bit of Wisdom:

Success seems to be connected with action. Successful people keep moving. They make mistakes, but they don't quit.

~ Conrad Hilton

25

Strategic Relations

There is an important section in my goal-setting book I call Strategic Relations. Another thing I learned from my strategic coach was to create my Top 20 Club. These are the top 20 relationships I have developed. This list can change based on activity. It is a list of my most important cases I am trying to close by the end of next quarter. These are my most immediate goals. These are tasks and cases that pay my bills over the next three months.

A Little Bit of Wisdom:

You have to perform at a consistently higher level than others. That's the mark of a true professional.

~ Joe Paterno

26

Farm Club

When I first started selling—I had what I called the farm club. These were people whom I was working with who I judged would become clients in the future. These were people who might become clients more than 90 days out. Not only should we focus on immediate income (top 20 club), but we must focus beyond 90 days as well. I still use the concept. These are prospects, but they haven't actually made the decision to move forward on my recommendations yet. They are important because I know from experience that if I continue to pursue them, a good percentage of them will convert into income for me and the company. For many agents, this kind of prospect is often forgotten and cast aside as a waste of time. They might just give up on them, but not me. My farm club is the people who others let slip through the cracks, but I work on them and eventually sell them.

As the late Sid Friedman, one my heroes, once said, "If you failed a million times, try a million and one times. Never ever give up." Dreaming, planning and discipline were his mantra and mine, as well.

One of my other favorite expressions in goal setting is, "If you have a good Monday you really can't have a bad week." Try to get off to a really good start at the beginning of the week. This sets your attitude and gives you the courage to face the rejection and problems that can occur during the week. If you start right, you actually increase the chance of having a really good week when it comes to meeting with existing and prospective clients and closing business.

27

Prospecting

Someone asked me once, "What is the life blood of the financial planning business?" What would you say? My answer was simple. I said, "It is prospecting, getting out there and getting in front of people." Prospecting, in my opinion, is more an art than a science. It is something you need to do every single day. For men, it is kind of like shaving. If you don't shave every day, pretty soon you're going to have a big, bushy beard. And unless you want to have a beard, you really need to make time to shave every single day.

A key to a positive attitude is keeping well groomed and manicured. You obviously don't want to look slovenly. Prospecting is the same thing. It needs to be done every single day in order to survive in this business. Remember, you can never prospect too much, just like you can never make too much money. And in my experience, prospecting is making money. Good prospecting is another way to say commissions. Please remember my friend: see more, sell more. The more people you see, the more sales you will make.

I know of colleagues in this business who are always prospecting no matter what they're doing or where they are. Regardless of the time of day or the social situation they are always sizing up someone and measuring them for business.

I am not like that. I stay away from being on after working hours. I only concentrate on prospecting during my allotted working time. This is a benefit to planning. I work when I work and play when I play.

Now don't get me wrong, I do keep alert during non-working time, but I'm not actively prospecting because I want some down time. I found I actually need some down time, some time away from the pressures of our business. I don't want to be on all the time. There's a time and place for everything. And as I just said, it's good to work hard and it's good to play hard—but you have to remember not to work hard and play hard during the same hours.

Let me give you some ideas I have used over the years to help me achieve my long track record of success. If you really knew how well I've built up my business, you would understand these ideas really do work. And you might be surprised to hear why I don't use many of them today. Well, the old expression is true, "it worked so well I stopped doing it." What do I mean by that? I would get so successful I would get bored and move on to another challenge. I moved beyond needing some of the tools that got me here.

For example, say you are an orthodontist and you have invested in all kinds of tools and equipment used to install and adjust braces. One day you discover a pill that patients can take once and suddenly all their teeth are in perfect alignment. Now you don't need your tools and equipment any more. You just moved to the next level and all of your equipment became obsolete. What was once the lifeblood of your business is no longer important to you. The same goes for some of the following ideas. Use them, and pretty soon you'll be so successful you won't need them any more—you will move on to a whole other array of more sophisticated tools.

28

The $2 Bill

I call this first idea the $2 bill. This idea started probably 25 years ago when I was working the professional market, going after attorneys for disability protection. I really didn't know how to open those doors.

As I mentioned earlier, I had become an expert in disability income insurance. Being an expert is great as long as you have prospects to tell your story to. This is what I did. I got hold of the county bar association directory in my local area. I randomly selected 20 names from the book. I called the offices of each person on my list. I wanted to make sure the address was up to date. By calling the office and speaking to the receptionist, I could verify that the attorney was still at the same address so I could send a pre-approach letter.

Then I would send a letter with a $2 bill attached to an enclosed letter. The letter said, "Dear Mr. Jones. Attached is a tax-free United States $2 bill. My name is Marc Silverman and I specialize in the area of disability income insurance. I'm going to be calling you for an appointment to discuss how you can receive more of these tax-free bills should you become sick or injured."

I would send out 20 of these every week. And the following week, I followed up with a phone call.

I said, "Is Mr. Jones there, please?"

"Who is this?"

"Marc Silverman. I am the gentlemen who sent him the $2 bill in the mail."

Once I got him on the phone, I would say the following: "I would like to come by and introduce myself and show you how you can get more of these tax-free bills if you were to become sick or injured in any capacity."

I sent these out every week. I usually sent them out on Thursdays and made the follow-up phone call the following

Tuesday. Well, my $2 bill generated a lot of activity for me and it generated a number of sales. It helped me acquire approximately 300 attorneys I still retain today as clients. Just imagine how many referrals I've gotten over the years from these clients. For only $40 a week, I have earned millions in commissions over the years. I think that's a pretty good investment, don't you?

So this is one idea that helped me get started in a new market. This is a very simple idea that anyone in any country can utilize in order to penetrate a new market. It doesn't have to be U.S. currency; it can be anything that grabs their attention so they remember you when you follow up with them.

The whole point of prospecting, in my opinion, is to be different, not do what everyone else is doing.

Another important benefit of the $2 bill for me was that it generated a lot of daytime appointments. It helped me fill my day with productive activity and left me more time in the evenings to either hold appointments or to enjoy my family.

29

Direct Mail

I did a lot of direct mail. Don't confuse direct mail with the $2 bill tactic. When I first started in the business back in 1983, there were a lot of agents doing direct mail. I think direct mail is much more saturated today, so I am not sure it works as well. But back then it did still work and I made a number of sales using direct mail.

Frankly, I found direct mail was not the best way to really generate new business. It cost a lot of money and can waste a lot of time. These replies had me running around at night trying to qualify prospects to see if I could make them clients. It really wasn't working as well for me as I would have liked.

I still have a lot of the clients I met through direct mail and I was able to generate all kinds of additional sales, be it life insurance and/or annuities and/or 401K sales. This was probably not the best use of my time, but it did keep me busy when I first got started.

A Little Bit of Wisdom:

You will never leave where you are, until you decide where you'd rather be.

~ Dexter Yager

30

Block of Wood Concept

Here is another concept that I used to help me open closed doors. After all why not make yourself different? I got the idea from an MDRT meeting. I went down to a lumber yard. I asked them to take a large sheet of ½ inch-thick plywood and cut it into the size of postcards. Then I bought Dun & Bradstreet lists of businesses in the area, businesses that fit my profile that I wanted to meet.

I picked businesses that had been in business between two and ten years. You don't want to go after a start-up business because they rarely have any money to do what they know they should do. If you try to find a well-seasoned business that's been around a long time, they are likely to already have established relationships with qualified financial services professionals.

What I did was to get stick-on labels and I put the name of the business and the address on the front of the wood with a stamp and my return address. On the back of the wood, I wrote the following, "I have ideas that are stronger than this!"

And I would simply call the following week after sending them out to the businesses. I would call Mr. Jones and say, "I'm the person who sent you the block of wood in the mail. I'm in the financial services business and I would like to stop by and introduce myself. I have a couple of ideas and concepts that I think you will find to be beneficial that I have shared with other successful business owners. Would Monday work for you or would Tuesday afternoon be better? This is a yes, yes close. Remember, your goal on the phone is to set a meeting and nothing more. This did work very well, to say the least. It worked so well that I stopped doing it.

That block of wood concept worked really well and got me into a lot of different companies and I wrote a lot of business. I successfully worked with the owners of Windjammer Cruise Services as a result of a block of wood and some creativity. All ideas will work as long as you are willing to try them and work yourself. Most people in our business unfortunately fail because they are not willing to give 100 percent.

I also did business with the second-largest modeling agency in the United States through a block of wood.

So being different and using little ideas like these will work, as long as you are willing to work. I took 20 $2 bills and ten blocks of wood and sent them out each week and this gave me an unlimited supply of people to call. When I made my follow-up phone calls people would not necessarily be at their place of business or able to take my call. So, the following week I would call back again and before you knew it I had a huge stack of people to call. And with a constant flow of leads, I was closing sales left and right.

31

Personal Observation

One of my favorite ways to prospect is through personal observation. This obviously involves taking a look at your surroundings, whom you do business with and how you come to work each day. You may want to try going to work a different way now and again and see if you discover anything that strikes you as being different. Try looking for a place where you might be able to work your way in.

Let me give you an example of personal observation. As a hobby I like aquariums and exotic fish. I have a very large saltwater fish tank in my home. I had an individual come to my house to take a look at my fish tank. The person who sold it to me was always calling and asking if he could bring his potential clients to my house to see the tank because it was a great showpiece and it was a great sales tool for him. He could show prospective customers an actual example of what it might look like to have a large aquarium in their own home or office.

One day, he brought a prospective customer to my house and the client looked at my fish tank. I recall it was a Saturday afternoon. I was in cut-off shorts and a T-shirt and we started talking. The client came up to my house driving his Rolls Royce. I notice little things like this and he liked the fish tank a lot.

This prospect spent an hour looking around and thinking about the tank. He finally said to me, "What do you do for a living? You have a beautiful home.

I said, "I'm in the financial services business."

He then told me he had just bought a $5 million life insurance policy last year. He told me he was in the process of selling this policy. I didn't quite understand what he meant at first. Then the light went on. This was back when someone could buy a policy and then sell it and make a profit.

Well, after weeping at the thought that this great prospect wouldn't be interested in my services, I gave him one of my business cards anyway and said, "If you ever need anything just give me a call."

That was on a Saturday. The following Wednesday, he called my office and one of my assistants said, "Mr. Smith is on the line."

I didn't know a Mr. Smith, so I said, "Who is Mr. Smith?"

She said, "He is the fellow who was at your house last Saturday."

I invited him to my office and we had lunch. He ended up purchasing a $5 million policy from me and two years later we rewrote the policy to $10 million. He ended up spending $350,000 a year in premiums. Now, that is what I mean by personal observation.

All of this happened as a result of me observing a situation and then looking for an opening. I created the opening by noticing the prospect's Rolls Royce. It was obvious he had money and as I said earlier, the higher the net worth of a prospect, the higher the income to you when you close the sale.

So be aware of your surroundings. Be aware of the people you are working with. Personal observation works really well when you leverage your relationships and situations to the next level.

Here is another personal observation concept anyone can use. When we were building our house, one of the contractors installed lights for us. They were landscaping lights set to shine on our trees. They were called property security lights. The owner of the company asked me what I did for a living. I told him I worked with clients as a financial planning expert. The next thing I knew he asked me to review his situation. It turned out he had a bunch of term insurance but was not physically in great shape. His health wasn't very good.

After reviewing the term policy, I got contracted with his insurance company and converted his term insurance to permanent insurance. This obviously was of great help to him and he was very grateful because he had not seen his agent for years. This happened because I was vigilant and put myself in a position to build a relationship with him. That's just thinking outside the box. He was just making polite small talk when he asked me what I did for a living, but I was thinking outside of the box from a sales perspective. It turned out quite well for me—and for him.

I love nice cars, very nice cars. The owner of the dealership where I purchase my cars is now a client. The salesperson who sold me my car is a client. You could call it lifestyle prospecting, but this happens frequently when you use personal observation as a way to identify opportunity.

Next time, when you are working with a company or person, look for an opening to start a conversation about business. Out of courtesy, they will usually ask you what you do. Now you can use your 3-minute elevator talk. But you have to ask or you are not going to get anywhere. I know that this seems obvious, but most people do not ask. If you do ask, they might say no, but they might also say yes. So you need to take the risk. And if you are experienced in selling, taking the risk of hearing no isn't much of a risk at all. It's just a way of life. It is SOP—standard operating procedure.

32

The Harder I Work the Luckier I Get

This is another old expression—the harder I work the luckier I get. Hard work always seems to pay off. It's that one extra phone call each day. It's working that one extra hour instead of going home early. It's getting into the office early in the morning. When I speak, agents will ask me, "Marc, what is your secret?"

As I mentioned earlier, I tell them, "I work half a day every day and it doesn't matter which 12 hours." So feel free to work half-days. It's doesn't matter when you start or when you end. But you have to work and pay the price. If you work 12 hours every day you work, you will be in good shape.

The other thing I do in my practice is to continuously look for opportunities. I like the phrase: think outside of the box.

Here's another story. I was invited to a wedding just recently in St. Augustine, Florida. I sat at a table with a dentist, an oral surgeon. After visiting for a while, it was obvious we had a lot in common. We had a good time getting to know one another.

He asked me what I did for a living. I explained what I did and he told me to call him when we both got back to Miami. He agreed to come by my office a week later. We spent some time together at my office. He is now a client. Personal observation does work.

33

Client Appreciation

This is one of the most under-utilized ways to build your business I know about. We do a lot of client appreciation events. Client appreciation events can come in different shapes and sizes. It might involve a really nice dinner at a great restaurant where you invite clients for nothing more than a get-together. It is an opportunity to thank them for their business and any referrals they have sent your way.

It is important to keep these events social. They are not sales seminars. They are not prospecting events. You don't talk business or products. It is simply a way of connecting with your clients on a different level than calling them and trying to sell them.

I have found that when I share a meal with someone I get to know that person on a completely different level than when I am in a selling situation. These client appreciation events work well. You might be thinking you can't afford to do this yet. But you don't need to spend a lot of money to do these events. It is entirely possible that you can get an insurance company to sponsor most of the event. This will help defray some of the cost. But don't forget to get approval from your broker/dealer as well as make sure you comply with the laws on advertising and marketing. Some of the restrictions are not logical and so you might not think you are violating any rules. It is always important to check to see if your event is within the compliance rules. The broker/dealer is your friend.

34

Love Affair Marketing

One of my favorite methods of marketing is what I call love affair marketing events. This is another form of client appreciation. Why not take your ten or fifteen best referral sources to dinner? I do this every year. We just recently held the dinner at a Ruth's Chris Steakhouse. I invited fifteen of our clients who have referred a lot of business to us during this last year. It was nothing more than a thank you for all their referrals and what they've done for us during the year. These dinners really build on the relationship with the client. They always seem to bring new business as well.

35

Other Marketing Ideas

We also will do an event at my country club each year. This is not a client appreciation event but a workshop instead.

One of the most popular is a workshop with one of the top money managers as the guest speaker. We invite our top clients who already have money with this manager. We also ask them to bring someone we have never met before. This has the potential of creating new marketing opportunities for us.

Think about it. You're doing an event at a country club. You're asking your existing clients to come in and hear an interesting speaker. They already like you and they bring someone along you don't know. This transfers their trust and confidence over to you. It is a natural way to build new relationships.

36

Hire Staff and Delegate the Role of Appointment-Making

One strategy that has worked extremely well for me is to have someone in my office make all of my appointments. We have to delegate as much of our routine tasks as possible. So I have an appointment setter. Nine years ago, I decided that I couldn't do everything myself. I only have 24 hours in a given day, just like you do. The one commodity we can never expand or replace is time. Yet, time management is key to running a successful business. Without good time management, you will fall way short of your potential.

I was really good on the phone. But I decided I needed to see if I could train someone to do this job effectively. That way, I could be seeing people instead of sitting in my office dialing for dollars. I mentioned I used to make phone calls from 9:00AM until 10:30AM trying to make appointments. That was time I could be doing something else. So now I have someone else do that job for me and I spend my time doing what I do best—selling.

Knowing how to delegate is really an art. There are not hard and fast rules. You must practice it, find the right people to delegate the right tasks to and make sure you put that saved time to good use by working on your business instead of in your business.

My telemarketer does all of my marketing for me and sets all of my appointments. She calls the people I identify as likely prospects for appointments, either new people or existing clients for annual reviews.

Her job is performance and is measured by two things. First, her goal is to set no less than 20 meetings each week and second, the appointments need to be quality appointments. It doesn't do me any good to have her set appointments that are a waste of time. This has really worked for me, because we see on average about 1200 people a year in my office. Do the math; this is about 100 a month or 25 a week. It is hard to fail when you are seeing this many people.

For a newer agent, having an appointment maker is a way to increase activity. If you make 100 sales a year and lose one, you have only lost about 1% of your earnings. But if you are only making 20 sales a year and you lose one, you've lost about 5% of your earnings. Newer agents should do whatever they can to make sure they are making at least 100 sales a year, more if possible. If you are making very few sales and you lose one, it's not good.

The same goes for prospecting and appointments. Lots of people cancel their appointments. It's just the nature of our profession—an occupational hazard, if you will. By only seeing four prospects a week and two cancel or defer to another week, you have lost 50% of your activity for the week. This can be terminal for many agents. In the beginning, activity is the key to success. I promise you, it does get easier and better with time.

So if you want to increase your chances of success and strive to reach top production levels, have 20 meetings a week. You may still lose three or four, but if you do, you will still have enough appointments to make your goals. Remember it is all in your metrics.

A by-product of having an appointment setter has been the relationships she has built. My clients have gotten to know her over the years and they are used to hearing from her. They expect her call. This makes setting appointments all that much easier.

Here is another prospecting tip. When clients call in, have your staff ask, "When does your next CD come due?" This is an automatic opportunity to gather assets into an annuity. By logging that information, it gives her an opening when she calls them back.

Let's assume you get a client on the phone who says, "Oh, I have a CD coming due next July," or in your interview process you discover the same thing. I'll plug it into my computer database and then either I will call or have my appointment setter call at the end of June.

When she calls in June she will say something like the following, "When we last spoke, you told me (us) you have a CD coming due next month. Let's get together and talk about it because

I have some ideas you may find of value. Let's turn your taxable dollars into tax-deferred dollars." This of course would be an annuity concept. The worst thing that client can say is no—but they may say yes.

This is just another form of observation prospecting. Using this technique is a great opportunity for you to follow up with your well-qualified client.

A Little Bit of Wisdom:

Snowflakes are one of nature's most fragile things, but just look at what they can do when they stick together.

~ Vesta Kelly

37

Invest In People to Help You

I have noticed through the years that agents are hesitant to invest in their office staff because they see it only as an expenditure of money, not an investment. But you have to look at it as leverage. You can only be in one place at one time and there are only 24 hours in your day. You have to make the most of your available hours. Ask yourself, where are you most profitable? Support staff helps you bring more to your bottom line.

Here is the question you need to ask while you read this book, can you pay someone to do many of the tasks you are doing now? If you can, then you shouldn't be doing what you pay someone else to do because your time is far too valuable.

For example, I admitted I thought I was the only one who could make phone calls for appointments. I thought I was the only one who could overcome their objections and secure the appointment.

When I hired my appointment setter approximately eleven years ago, I discovered she was equally adept. She could make all of the same phone calls and set just as many appointments. Once I understood this and embraced it, my business really soared. I didn't believe anyone else could do it. Today, she is responsible for setting up meetings for me and two other producers who work in our office. She is great at her job.

She does it all. She sets up new appointments. She sets up annual reviews. She sets up telephone conference calls. These are her main responsibilities.

She is compensated with a salary and she's also compensated for each qualified appointment that actually shows up to my office. There is a tangible, motivating reward for her success.

The more appointments she makes, the more money she earns. We are both working for the same goal. She also is responsible for setting up all of our workshops. She sets up her schedule in January and by the end of January, we usually have appointments and workshops established for March and April. That's how effective she is.

She's responsible for getting letters approved by the insurance company's compliance department, making sure our Web site is up to date by getting it compliance approved. She handles the mailings, the e-mail drip system to contacts in our database. In a nutshell, she is the marketing arm of my business. The key to having someone like her work for you is to treat her fairly, respectfully, and professionally. You can motivate your appointment setter through a creative and generous compensation arrangement.

I call her the mainspring of my business. She powers the watch and keeps it all ticking. Without her I would have a real problem. I would have to do everything she does and my job as well. She is a great asset and has grown into being a vital member of the team. Frankly, I don't know what I would do without her.

By the way, I did not just decide to hire her one day and point her towards a phone, a desk and a computer, not at all. I worked with her extensively. I trained her and role-played with her. We went through all the objections she was likely to encounter. We dealt with objections such as "no need, no money, no wants and no hurry." It did not take her long until she was confident and capable to effectively set appointments and start a flow of prospects coming into our office.

Today, she is setting up these meetings for annual reviews on a regular basis. They all know her now. Most clients have spoken with her multiple times. She is not a cold voice calling a total stranger. She is the heart of our marketing system.

I would encourage you to invest some money in your business and hire someone to schedule meetings to make appointments for you. If you do it right and train them and take care of that person, your return-on-investment will be many times over.

A Little Bit of Wisdom:

Life's blows cannot break a person whose spirit is warmed at the fire of enthusiasm.

~ Norman Vincent Peale

38

EZ Data

In addition to my marketing person, we have a receptionist who, when you walk in the office, is responsible for putting all of my audits together before I see a client or prospect. This is a big job and there is a lot to do. We are notorious note takers in the office. We use a software program called EZ Data. It is a client database system for tracking all of our activity. I liken our office to a doctor's office. When you first go to a doctor's office you are given a clip board and an intake questionnaire. You are asked to fill out everything you can about yourself along with all your medical history, family history and any significant illnesses.

We have tried to duplicate this process in our office. When a prospect comes into our office the first thing we do is have a detailed fact-finder filled out. This is an absolute requirement. Once it is completed, I start talking to them and I take notes. This all gets dictated into the phone (I use a service called copytalk for my dictation) and then it is e-mailed back to us. It is copied and pasted into the client's file and tagged to the notes.

The EZ Data system is compliance approved and it backs itself up every few minutes. I highly recommend it—it's been an invaluable tool.

39

Don't Count on Your Memory

Here is a good rule to follow—document everything. Memory is a dicey tool and you should not rely on it. No matter how good you think your memory is, you need to keep meticulous records. When a client returns to my office six months later, my receptionist prints off the last set of notes so I can review them before the meeting. She also organizes and provides me with an updated audit so I know exactly what products this client owns. There is nothing worse than looking like you don't know what is going on with a client's portfolio.

I can walk into any meeting, with any client and know everything about that person's situation as it should be. This is saying a lot because I have thousands of clients. I can review the last set of notes that were taken and know exactly what was done. I know exactly what was discussed because it is part of our process and we follow our process. It is required that we take notes so we have a detailed outline of everything discussed and implemented.

If you are seeing 100 people a month, you do not want to trust just your memory. I admit, note taking is labor-intensive and requires dedication and discipline. It forces you to concentrate. Your mind can't wander if you have trained yourself to take good notes.

Remember what I said earlier about cold calling? That you can calculate how much each cold call is worth based on the number of cold calls you make and the amount you earn each year? Well, the same can be said for taking notes. Count up the number of pages of notes you take in a year and divide that number into your income for that same period. If you take 1,000 pages of notes and earn $150,000—then each page of notes is worth $150 to you. Do you think it is worth $150 to take that page of notes? That should take some of the sting out the tedium and effort required to make this effort.

40

Statements of Understanding

Unfortunately, the regulators don't like annuities. So we are very cautious to make sure we document every conversation with our clients. We want them to sign a disclosure and approval letter. It is what we call our Statement of Understanding. We use this statement of understanding to make sure the client clearly understands every contractual element of the annuity and the implications. Clients seem to remember what they want. I call this selective memory when the market is not performing well. We want full disclosure to protect us and our clients. Of course, we submitted the statement of understanding for approval from our compliance department.

The client understands everything in the contract, the surrender charges, mortality expense, the investment loads and distribution options. By signing it, they acknowledge we have told them everything about the contract and they understand what we have told them. That way, the client can't come back to us three years later when the markets are down and say, "Well you know, I never understood that I couldn't cash out the guaranteed portion of the annuity."

Because I am so careful to explain every aspect of the annuity, including all the risks, I rarely have a client who complains about how the stock market has impacted their retirement plan.

And if they do come back and question our recommendation, we say. "Well, wait a minute. We discussed that with you in detail. We have the statement you signed acknowledging we went through that provision with you. What part of this did you not understand?" We are very, very cautious to document these conversations.

41

The Little Details Make a Big Difference

As you can tell—I am a stickler for detail. I like process and I want every aspect of our organization running smoothly. An example of this is my receptionist. Among her many duties, she is responsible for making sure we are hospitable. She is in charge of the coffee. Whether it is regular coffee, decaf, tea, cappuccino, espresso, or latte, whatever the client likes, we have it ready.

It may sound silly, but we make a note of what our clients like and how they like it. We keep this information in the computer. So when clients come into the office, we don't have to ask them what they want. We just ask if they'd like what they had last time. It is a nice added touch that makes us a little bit different than most other offices. Paying attention to the little details makes a huge positive impact to our bottom line.

You should see the reactions when our receptionist says, "You like your coffee black with two sugars, right?"

"Wow! What a memory!" But it's not memory; it's observation and note taking.

Everyone in the office makes an effort to be super-friendly to anyone who comes in. All we have to sell is our relationship with them. We can have the best products, but if they don't like us, they will do business someplace else. Perception is everything. Treat your clients like gold, it will pay off.

42

Answer By the Second Ring

Here is another little detail, but it is important. I absolutely require my receptionist and anyone else in our office to answer the phone by the second ring. I don't want people calling in and waiting and going through voicemail and doing all the other crazy things that have dehumanized our world. I want a live human being answering the phone. I believe if you provide unparalleled service—which all starts with your office staff—the clients will start chasing after you.

Now, don't get me wrong. We do make mistakes and miss things. Absolutely. But we try to recognize our mistakes and fix them. I think we get it right more than we get it wrong and that's one of the main reasons we do the business we do. You can't be perfect, but through hard work you can minimize your imperfect qualities.

A Little Bit of Wisdom:

We are what we repeatedly do. Excellence, then, is not an act, but a habit.

~ Aristotle

43

Promote Your Staff to Key Positions

One of my staff who started out as a receptionist, wanted to become a certified financial planner. She is bright and does an excellent job for the firm and our clients.

Over time, her responsibilities segued from being the receptionist to being in charge of seeing clients to conduct their annual review. I believe annual reviews are incredibly important. Whenever you can see a client on a positive basis, do it. Clients should get used to working with your staff and dealing with someone other than you. I know you think you are indispensible. But that attitude is what keeps most producers from really growing.

I introduce new clients to my staff and pass them off to the appropriate persons so they are not dependent upon me and calling for every little thing that needs to be done. Otherwise, every time a client needs to do something, you are going to end up being on the phone taking care of service issues—and you make more money selling than servicing. Please don't forget this. Don't get me wrong. Service is essential, but who delivers the service is the issue. You can provide excellent service by using qualified staff. It doesn't have to be you.

So let your clients know who in your office will handle any questions they might have regarding the Web site or monthly statements or premium notices. If you set up the expectations properly in the beginning, you can free yourself to do what you do best; see the people.

One of my office staff assistants works beside me. She takes care of almost all the applications and does many of the client meetings for annual reviews and fact-finding with new clients as well. Whenever possible, always promote from within. It's win-win for your entire office.

Little Bit of Wisdom:

Success is the maximum utilization of the ability that you have.

~ Zig Ziglar

44

Follow Through and Follow Up

My assistant is also great at follow through and follow up. You need at least one person on your staff who can fulfill your promises. I believe you've got to have a follow-up and follow-through system in place in order to catch sales you might otherwise miss. These sales will often fall through the cracks.

Here is a sale I made recently by having a follow-up system in place. I called a prospect just to follow up on our last appointment several weeks earlier. When he got on the phone he said to me, "You know, I've been meaning to call you, but I've never gotten around to it." Then he said to me, "Yeah, I'd like to move forward with your suggestions." A few days later we picked up a $90,000 check. Just because I took a few seconds to dial a number from the list of people I needed to make sure didn't disappear from my farm club. It's the follow-up and follow-through systems that make these kinds of sales not only possible—but probable.

My assistant nags me to make sure I do follow up with the clients and prospects who need a call. She's really invaluable. She also reads a lot of articles and will bring items to my attention if she thinks we need to discuss them.

I mentioned we did a dinner event to thank those people who have referred us a lot of business. Remember, this dinner was not about selling, it is a client appreciation dinner.

One of the people at the dinner said, "I've had it with my employer, I'm going to retire." He came in to see me a few days later and we filled out all of his retirement paperwork. I had been working with him for a number of years preparing him for retirement. I had not done any business with him up to this point. You must start the relationship in order to ultimately get new business. This may seem obvious, but not a lot of people do this. Most salespeople want instant gratification. He is now going to retire in about six months. I worked with him on his retirement plan and he liked it and told me to implement it. Just that one sale paid for the client appreciation dinner several times over.

A Little Bit of Wisdom:

Our greatest glory, is not in never failing, but in rising up every time we fail.

~ Ralph Waldo Emerson

45

Create To-Do Lists

I track my obligations by using a to-do list. I'm kind of old fashioned this way. I could keep it on the computer and pull it up every day. But I like to have it staring in front of me and I write down the names of the individuals and what I need to do to finalize my recommendations for them.

Then I go back to the computer and look up their name and review their record. I get all the details I need in order to do an effective job with my follow up.

Fortunately, I'm so busy most of the time, if someone I am working on fails to act, I usually just move on to the next name. But if things get a little slow or I have a spare minute I'll pick up the follow-up list and start making some phone calls.

> **Silverman-ism:**
> **People don't plan to fail financially, they just fail to plan.**

46

Hire Knowledgeable People

Having a great staff makes all the difference. One thing that works for me is to hire people who know the businesses and companies we're trying to develop as clients. We do a lot of work with several major utility companies, government organizations and phone companies. A couple of years ago, when I saw the huge sales potential among employees at a large south Florida telephone company, I hired a marketing person who had just retired from the phone company and was a client of ours.

She knew how to get into all of the phone company offices. We hired her to place fliers announcing our upcoming financial planning workshops. She had access and helped communicate with many more employees than if we had done it ourselves.

I believe you need to take care of your office. I believe you need to treat your employees and colleagues with respect and obviously do right by them. It's so much harder to replace someone who has been with you a number of years than to start all over again with someone new. It's much easier to keep someone by trying to meet their financial and security needs.

In addition to my assistant, I also have one main office support person. She had been with me for 11 years. She is my office manager and she really runs the office. She pays all the bills and supports me in all of our life insurance business activities.

She does most of the follow ups by taking care of all the letters, she coordinates my personal travel plans and generally gets the things done I don't want to do on a daily basis. She does a great job tying up the loose ends.

47

Rationale for Hiring a Marketing/Lead-Generating Person In Your Office

I just don't have time anymore to spend an hour and a half every day contacting or trying to make appointments. What I'm able to do is have someone in the office do it for me.

When I realized this, I decided I had to delegate my marketing. Now I can just walk into the office and I'm fully booked. I'll give you a good example of why this works so well.

Most of us take vacations. When we go on a vacation, it is easy to become distracted the week before we leave. Then we are gone and it usually takes about a week to catch up when we get back. So, in reality, we just took a three-week vacation. That was how it was for me.

I don't operate like this anymore because I'm fully booked up until the time I leave. I'm gone for the week and when I get back I have a full slate of appointments waiting for me. All because I have somebody making appointments for me.

As an example, my wife and I were out of the country for the last week of November. When I came back the following week, I had 19 meetings scheduled and the week before I left, I had 14 meetings in three days. Little things like this make a huge difference.

This is essential if you want to move to higher levels of production. You need someone who makes your appointments and does your marketing. It certainly makes things a lot easier to stay productive.

48

Using the Web

The other way we prospect is through the Internet, the Web. We have a very nice Web site and people can make appointments to see us directly on our site. We advertise our workshops on our Web site and we always get a number of people who will attend the workshop because they saw it promoted there. It is incredible to me, how many people go online and look at our Web site. It is an important marketing tool.

Here is another great way to market your services. Stay in touch with clients and prospects via e-mail once a month. I hired a professional writer to do my newsletter. If you try this, don't forget to get it approved by the insurance company's compliance department each month.

For example, we're working with a writer who also writes for the Wall Street Journal. He has written a number of books and writes e-mails containing financial planning articles of interest for our clients.

For example, gold is getting a lot of headlines. Is gold the right commodity to be purchasing? He has written some great articles for our client newsletter. And, again, this is one more touch point—it is our way of staying in touch with clients on a regular basis with very little effort or expense. It is worth the time.

49

Referrals

I have always asked for referrals, but I do it in a roundabout way today. Referrals are the life blood of a good practice because they come from someone who knows you, likes you and trusts you. Those three main ingredients must be prevalent for you to be successful in any sales situation.

There are many different ways to ask for referrals but mainly, you just have to ask. If you're afraid to ask you're not going to get any. The worst thing that can happen is that you'll get a no. But you'll be surprised how often just asking for a referral will net you at least one—or maybe even two or three.

Here is a simple referral statement I make that has worked effectively.

"Joe, I really appreciate that you decided to become a client and hopefully you're happy with the service we have provided for you. My business relies on seeing new people and most people in my business spend 80% of their time looking for new people and 20% of their time servicing their clientele. We have reversed this. We spend 80% of our time working with clients and 20% of our time looking for new business, but in order to keep this model I need your help. I mean I really need your help. Would you be kind enough to provide us with people you know who might be interested in the same services you have received through us?"

Sometimes, you have to feed and tell. To find people to ask for referrals, go through your recent fact sheets and look for people who you really liked and connected with. Their fact sheets often divulge names or opportunities. You'll be amazed at the number of referrals you can pick up by saying:

"Joe, you mentioned you have a CPA. Can you tell me a little bit about your CPA?" Or you might say, "Your next door neighbor is so and so." Or you can say, "I remember you telling me that you're in the XYZ business. Who are your competitors? Would any of them be a good person for me to call and meet?" Keep in mind those competitors may be friendly with your client. You never know till you ask.

50

Referral List

I think you can be too aggressive sometimes, asking for referrals. So if I want to back off a little, I sometimes say, "If you're happy with the services we've provided, please don't keep us a secret. Tell your friends, relatives and any colleagues you know who might benefit from what we do and how we do it."

I had a husband and wife come into my office the other day. He had never met me before but was referred to me by someone I met at the airport in Miami.

This person came in to see me. He laid his cards on the table immediately. "Look, I'll be honest with you. My wife and I have met with two other financial planners. We just don't trust anyone right now. However, those planners were not referred to us, you were." This is an example of how a referral gives you a huge advantage.

We met for three hours and I was able to get their trust and respect, as well as their business. A referral is a transfer of trust and confidence. When you get a name, or someone calls, you already have the beginning of a great relationship. Why are they better-qualified prospects? Number one, they were referred to us and number two, they are coming to my office (so I know they are serious). Number three, we spend quite a bit of time to make them feel good about their potential retirement plan.

I'm not saying we sell all of our referrals, but we do get a lot of them and I think if you work hard on getting your clients to refer you business, it just makes you that much more effective.

51

Ask Around

If I am out and about, another technique I use is to see what is going on around me. Let's say you are calling on someone in the landscape maintenance business. You can go to the Yellow Pages and get a list of other landscape-related firms he might know or do business with. Write them down and take them with you on your appointment.

While you are on the appointment with the landscape prospect, say to him at an appropriate time, "I am going to be calling these 15 landscape architects I have identified as successful in our area. Do you happen to know any of them? Can you tell me anything about these people? Would you have any objection if I mentioned to them I am working with you?"

Feed and tell is a powerful way to identify potential prospects. These are people you might not meet any other way.

52

Unparalleled Service

I believe if you and your office staff provide unparalleled service to your clients, pretty soon the "fish will start chasing the boat." By unparalleled service, I mean the little things. I told you I am a stickler for answering the phone by the second ring. Having extensive knowledge of your clients' personal, financial, and professional lives is a way of telling them you care. Keeping in touch and following up whenever appropriate is yet another way. You need to do what you say you're going to do. As my good friend Sid Friedman used to say, "Under promise and over deliver" and "If it isn't broke, break it and make it better."

The point is, if you provide unparalleled service, if you do what most people are not willing to do, you're going to stand out from the crowd. I believe that this makes all the difference in the world.

53

Be Passionate

Be passionate about whatever it is that you're doing. I believe passion more than anything else helps you sell successfully.

I'll never forget taking a course at the University of Miami in marketing and sales. We had to give a three-minute presentation on the features, advantages and benefits of whatever the product was that we were selling.

After I made my three-minute presentation, my professor—who gave me an A-plus in the class—said, "Marc, I don't know what you were selling but I know I would have bought it." That's because I was selling with great passion and enthusiasm.

It's enthusiasm that sells. Enthusiasm comes from believing in your promises and your ability to deliver. Look at your track record and get excited about what you have already done. Then go out and do a lot more of it.

A Little Bit of Wisdom:

The secret of getting ahead is getting started.
~ *Mark Twain*

54

50 Hours Per Sale = a Successful Insurance Sales Professional

The average successful life insurance producer invests, all told, approximately 50 hours making one sale.

If you haven't been in the business that long, then a lot of those 50 hours goes into prospecting. The more seasoned you are, the more time you spend selling because you have developed a pretty good prospecting system. Fifty hours of work equals about one sale per week.

That's a lot of lot of work hours—but it's worth it. The industry average of 50 lives per year is what a successful life insurance sales person achieves.

So if you want to make 100 sales, you need to double your time. Since time is finite, there is only one solution, delegation. Extraordinary success in our business always comes back to one thing, effective time utilization. Find ways to expand your time.

55

Prospect Where You Play

One of the other ways you can prospect is through a country club. I realize not everyone is going to belong to a country club, but if you are a member of a country club it's a great way to do some prospecting. A health club, service club, or other organization can serve the same purpose. I do belong to a country club in Miami and I have many, many clients there.

I don't aggressively prospect at the country club, but people know what I do for a living. If someone asks me, I will obviously get together with them.

As Willie Sutton said when they asked him why he robbed banks, "It's because that's where the money is." Well, there's a lot of money in country clubs. Consider joining one if you don't already belong and spend some time there. People will pick up on what you do for a living. And that's the first step in getting referrals or meeting new clients.

Take a look at the hobbies, organizations, and activities you enjoy doing yourself. Similar interests create unique opportunities to discover built-in common ground with others. This is another important element for getting someone to trust you. It is another way for you to find people who are possible prospects.

56

Centers of Influence

COIs—centers of influence are another way to identify and approach business opportunities. As you begin to develop these centers of influence—people who see you as their go-to person for problem solving—you will find wonderful new opportunities to do business.

For example, there's an attorney in Miami who's an estate planning attorney. We have become fairly friendly over the years. I look for reasons to go back and visit with him. I always try to bring a good idea that might benefit one or more of his clients. I never know if I will hit a nerve with him. I like being able to continue our relationship.

About a month ago, he called me. "Hi, Marc. Your lucky day has arrived."

I said, "What are you talking about?"

He said, "I have a client who's worth $180 million. She wants to buy life insurance."

That was good news indeed. He arranged a meeting and I began working on what would be a very large sale. Will I get it? I don't know. But you can't hit a home run, unless you get to bat. So I am in the process of working on it. Will I work on it tirelessly and do everything I possibly can to close that sale? Absolutely. We live in a world based on the law of large numbers. So you never know what will happen, but you have to have confidence it will happen.

I know for a fact, other producers are not getting in front of estate planning attorneys. As a result, they have zero chance of making a sale like this one. Opportunities like this just don't fall into our laps. We have to actively find ways to make them—just as I do when I call up the estate planning attorney and meet with him to give him ideas. I help him, he helps me. And it pays off. Anyone can find centers of influence and create a relationship.

Some of my biggest cases have been the result of relationships just like this one. Make the time to identify centers of influence in your area and find ways to get in front of them, consistently. That way you are giving yourself a chance to get to bat.

To hit a home run you have to be on the team and on the field. Then you have to step up to the plate—but if you're never at the plate then there's no chance you will ever hit a home run.

A Little Bit of Wisdom:

What counts is not necessarily the size of the dog in the fight – it's the size of the fight in the dog.

~ Dwight D. Eisenhower

57

Get Involved In Industry Activities

I can't say this enough, getting involved in the industry is a great way to grow your business. You may ask, "What does getting involved in the industry have to do with prospecting?" The answer is simple: by being involved with MDRT, or finding speaking opportunities, or industry workshops, you get to listen to other people. I learn from all of them and I've picked up all kinds of prospecting ideas by being involved in and by attending industry activities. Prospecting is more than just looking for someone to talk to; it is also looking for something to talk about. Being involved keeps you fresh and excited. Try it, you'll like it.

A Little Bit of Wisdom:

The greatest thief this world has ever produced is procrastination, and he is still at large.

~ H.W. Shaw

58

Words of Tony Gordon

Maybe you have heard of Tony Gordon. Let me tell you a little bit about him. He is one of my heroes in the business.

Tony Gordon was the 2001 MDRT president. He is a 32-year MDRT member from Bristol, England, and he's a 31-year Top of the Table qualifier. Gordon has served MDRT and other industry associations and numerous leadership positions. He's a bestselling author and speaks to industry audiences throughout the world. We were on the same platform in Shanghai and again at the annual MDRT in Anaheim, California. Tony told audience members there is only one reason anyone fails in the insurance business. It is the one reason and one reason only, it is lack of discipline.

He said "Successful people discipline themselves to do the things unsuccessful people don't like to do." For example, at the beginning of each week on Monday, Tony says he decides how many calls he is going to make and he doesn't go home Friday until they're done. And this is a guy who is incredibly successful, but he still sets his call goals, and still sticks to them.

It does not matter what level of success you have attained in this business—it will always be this week's activities that make next week's commissions. You simply cannot separate this week's action from next week's sales.

Although I have achieved a high level of success as a financial planner, I know one thing for sure. I still need to keep learning. Tony Gordon is one of my mentors. I recently flew him to Miami to spend a day with me. I wanted his coaching. He flew in one Friday night, we had a great dinner and Saturday we spent all day in my office. He was mentoring and coaching me. On Sunday, he flew back to the U.K. It was worth every cent.

59

Find a Financial Planner Better Than You and Become Friends

Here's another prospecting method. Find people who are better than you in this business and start talking to them. Get to know them. Ask them what they do and how they do what they do. Listen carefully and you can learn from them. That's the exact reason I brought in Tony Gordon in last year.

> **A Little Bit of Wisdom:**
> **There is no chance, no destiny, no fate, that can hinder or control the firm resolve of a determined soul.**
> *~ Ella Wheeler Wilcox*

60

Marketing Your Business

How do you go about marketing your business?

It is easy to forget the difference between selling and marketing. In our business most sales people are so focused on selling they forget how to market themselves. Unless you market yourself effectively, you will always be doing it the hard way. Focusing only on selling reduces your influence and can actually make it tougher to make sales.

Fifty percent or more of our business results from marketing ourselves to other people. Sometimes I liken us to a frustrated actor, one who is a great actor but just can't get himself in front of a decent audience. You may be really good at presenting your story, but if you don't have an audience, you can be the best actor in the world, but no one cares. The same is true in selling. If you have no people to present your ideas to, you obviously can't make a sale.

61

Get Your Name Out There

You've got to have a systematic way of getting your name out to the public. You need a way of getting in front of people on a favorable basis.

If you can't get in front of people in a favorable setting, what good is all your knowledge, experience and presentation skills? How do you market yourself to the public? How do you market yourself so the fish will start chasing the boat instead of the boat always chasing the fish?

One way is to start with affinity groups, groups of people who have common interests, even common employers, for example.

At my company, we have marketed ourselves to employees at the local phone companies, the local utility companies and through the Florida Retirement System. These are people who work for the state of Florida.

We do this by setting up workshops and appreciation dinners. We ask them to bring their friends and to get ready to learn something that will be valuable to them in their retirement. We consistently drip market on them to create awareness.

A Little Bit of Wisdom:

What you get by achieving your goals is not as important as what you become by achieving your goals.

~ *Zig Ziglar*

62

Target Marketing

Another form of affinity marketing is target marketing. These are groups of people who are affiliated with each other, people who have something in common besides their employer. Associations are a good example of targets. They all belong because they are in the same industry.

I am now looking more for affiliated groups of people than people who are unrelated. It's easier to target a group of people with similar interests than it is to try to do business with individuals. The linkage is what drives marketing.

Close one sale in a group, and others are likely to follow. And if that happens, chances are those subsequent sales will be a little easier because they were referred to you by a client from within that same group of affiliated people.

I'm not sure why, but I never believed in target marketing until I actually started doing it. Once I started to target market, my income started to soar. I liken it to a surgeon who goes from being a general surgeon to a specialist. Specialists always earn a lot more.

If you were having brain surgery, would you go to a general surgeon or a specialist? Obviously, you'd go to the one who has done the exact procedure many, many times before. You don't want them learning on you.

By getting affiliated with a group, you learn the ins and outs of that group and their special needs. Once you close a sale, one person tells another person and the word starts to spread positively. This can happen in an unbelievable way and really help market your business. Specialization and affiliated group marketing is definitely the way to go.

63

Workshops

I am a big believer in workshops. This is one of the best ways to prospect. Workshops are special events—in this case, events for prospective clients where you focus on specific topics of interest to those people who are in your target market.

And there are a couple of things I would mention when talking about workshops or whatever you label them. You are leveraging your time. Anytime you can tell your story to 30 people rather than two people, you've got a greater opportunity to make the sale. Which makes more sense, telling your idea to one or two people or to a whole group? When you plan your workshop, be sure to do whatever is necessary to get a decent audience. Plus, the more people you have in a room, the greater the energy within the group. It also gives you greater energy. If you do it right, you can have people lining up to make appointments with you because they want to learn more about your idea and hopefully they will want to buy.

64

Sell Yourself

Your ultimate objective with any workshop is to sell yourself. That's really why you are doing a workshop in the first place. It is unrealistic to think you are going to do a transaction in the workshop, right? You are the commodity you are marketing. You are selling them on coming to see you in your office for a one-on-one appointment. When you get them into your office, you have the home court advantage. You have a much better chance of winning their confidence and ultimately making them a client.

65

How to Develop Workshops

Agents often ask me how I created a workshop. Where did you get your material? They want to know the advantages and disadvantages of doing them. They also want to know if all the effort is worth it.

After working the disability and life insurance market for several years, I realized I wanted to get into the financial planning business rather than staying purely in the life insurance business. I was told workshops were a great way for me to network myself and tell my story. But I didn't have a curriculum.

The first thing I tell agents is, build your own workshop. You need to build your own story and your own slides. If you buy a turnkey slide show, it is not really your material. I think it is harder for you buy into the value and merit of your program if you are borrowing from someone else. If you build your own, then you have confidence in the story and you have pride of authorship. You will buy into it more and you will communicate it with real sincerity. It's much, much better to design your own workshop. You'll present the information much more convincingly.

66

When to Hold a Workshop

A lot of technical questions pop up when you're conducting workshops. Like, which is the best day of the week to hold them? Where do I purchase my workshop materials and handouts? What if someone in the audience knows more than I do? How long should the workshop last? Who do I believe when I read books written about how to create a workshop?

One of the best books on this subject was written by Frank Maselli. It's called, *Create Your Own Workshop/Create Your Own Numbers.*

I think Maselli's got some great ideas in his book, but based on my experience, I don't see how he gets the number of people to come into his office and meet with him. So don't be blown away by his results. I just accept the numbers he mentions, but pay attention, close attention to his ideas and concepts.

What days work best? I hold workshops on Tuesdays and Thursdays. Mondays don't work. They are the beginning of the week and people really don't want to attend a workshop after just coming back from the weekend. Fridays are lost as well. People are already gone, mentally. The end of the week is not a good day. I am ambivalent on Wednesdays. They are the middle of the week which may or may not work, but I find Tuesdays and Thursdays work best.

What time works best? This depends entirely on your audience. If you're working with seniors, you might want to hold it at 4:30PM and then serve dinner at 6:30PM. Yes, we serve dinners at our workshops. Everyone says, don't buy your attendance. They are not at super-fancy places and they don't cost a lot, but I feel it is important to give value. We hold them at places that are convenient and comfortable. We try to find a quiet, private room where we can hold these events.

The time that I find works best for people who are working is generally 6:30PM. If we are working with school teachers, we move it up a bit to 5:30PM. That works best. I talk to the audience for about an hour. I don't usually spend any more than this because they will lose focus and stop paying attention. Then we serve dinner and I work the room by talking to everyone. I try to connect with them in a personal way and encourage them to come into the office.

67

What to Talk About

What do I talk about in my workshops?

First, do some research. If you want to do workshops, read every author you can find who has a track record of success in the workshop business. But don't necessarily believe everything you read. In other words, take a little bit of this and a little bit of that. Use what resonates and sounds like it works. Then put it into your own format, your own way of getting things done.

I believe a lot of the people who write these books are in the business of selling books. I don't know that they really want to help you as much as get you to buy their books. I know that sounds cynical, but it comes from having read most of them and having done seminars for many years.

As I mentioned earlier, design and build your own workshop. For example, if you want to target your local phone company, you may want to build a workshop based around their pension plan or something else you know will be of current interest to them.

If you're holding a workshop for the public, most people who come to those workshops, especially if you're doing it for seniors, are there for the free dinner. I would say out of every 30 people who show up, 20 or more are there just for the free dinner. You might have a few people who are interested in listening, but mostly you have very few people who are interested in coming in to see you. Some of these folks are on the free-food seminar circuit. No kidding, they are real pros. We had someone call our office to see what we were going to serve.

Once you commit to workshops, you have got to keep doing them. I liken workshop marketing to fishing. When you go fishing, you never know what you're going to catch, but you have to go fishing in order to catch a fish. So you have to get out there and you have to do it.

If you're hosting a workshop and inviting the general public—as opposed to a workshop for an affiliated group—you should focus on subjects that matter to them. Make sure you are professionally interesting as well. I was taught by a colleague that you need to answer one question when putting together material: why would people want to come in and see me? What makes me different from the rest?

What information am I giving them that's going to entice them to come in and see me? What am I offering that is unique and different? What is going to encourage them to make an appointment to see me after the workshop is finished? What makes me special?

These are the questions you need to answer as you build your workshop. I once hosted a workshop for schoolteachers. I asked myself, "What should I talk to them about?" For me it was sharing about what was important to them. I had to have a reason for them to come and see me. The reason for them to come was simply to learn more about their pension plan, their 401K and the retirement process the school system used when they were ready to retire. I need to deliver information to them they otherwise do not know. That's how I earn their respect and gain their trust and ultimately earn their business.

68

How to Get Them to Come

One of the best ways we got people to come to our workshops was to hire someone who had retired and knew the problems and opportunities. We did this with a woman who had retired from the phone company. We gave her a list of all the county public schools, as an example. The list contained all the schools in the area where I wanted to establish my marketing presence.

Then I helped her create a promotional flyer discussing the Florida Retirement System. To do this, I had to go online and learn everything I could about the Florida Retirement System. My wife works in the system, so I already knew a little bit about it. But I did not know enough. So I was able to get on their Web site and learn everything I could about the retirement system.

Next, we dropped flyers at the various schools. We announced a dinner we were sponsoring. People responded to our flyer and came to the dinner. I told them about our exclusive IPRO (Independent Personal Retirement Overview). This is simply a fact-finder we use to help us get to know the financial issues for each teacher who comes to the office.

When they do come in, we use the IPRO to gather as much data as possible on them. We keep the fact-finding information on a file in our database and when they ultimately get ready to retire, we work with them and discuss their retirement options. We also invest new money they might have. When I first started doing workshops, most of that business came from this type of workshop. It gave us qualified leads and then I used my sales skills, knowledge and experience to close those sales. Workshops have always given us highly qualified leads.

You can learn more about workshop selling from your colleagues as well. Richard Sullinger does a great job utilizing workshops. Don Speakman has been doing workshops for 25 years and has really done a great job. I have learned a lot from both of these individuals. So I would like to thank both of them, publicly in this book.

69

What to Serve and Not Serve at a Workshop

We never serve alcohol at a workshop. I believe you need to keep alcohol out of your seminar entirely.

We tried to customize our events and not serve dinner. Instead, we served soft drinks and hors d'oeuvres. However, the cost of doing finger food wasn't much different than going to a restaurant and offering a fixed-price dinner for $25.00 a person. We decided we might as well spend the money serving dinner rather than doing appetizers.

The number of qualified appointments we booked was virtually the same either way we did it. But serving dinner was classier and bought us better PR with our seminar attendees. An added benefit was having everyone seated at the same time. It gave me another opportunity to address them when I could get their attention.

When you create your own workshop, you will probably experiment with different styles and approaches. Continue doing this until you find one that works best for you. We did this with the option of serving dinner or offering appetizers. We saw we were accomplishing the exact same thing, so why not go with the higher satisfier. That's what we found worked best, through trial and error. You will find what works for you.

70

What to Wear

What do I wear when I do a workshop? I dress casually. I wear a pair of dress slacks and a sports jacket. I wear a nice dress shirt. I don't wear a tie anymore. I find dressing down a little makes the atmosphere more relaxed and fun for the audience. It is much more casual and the audience enjoys the seminar more.

71

Who Attends From the Office?

One question which comes up often is who from my office staff attends the workshops. I try to not overwhelm the audience with my staff. So only my marketer, who I mentioned earlier, comes along with one financial planner who attends so she can gain experience, meet the prospects, and develop her own clients.

I think if you have too many there, it is intimidating for the attendees and makes them ask questions that are unnecessary. They can draw all sorts of conclusions if there is too much overhead involved with the seminar. Keep it simple but elegant.

72

How Many Should You Invite?

This is a common question. How many should you invite to a workshop? I don't like to have any more than 25 to 30 in a room. Some people argue you could have 100 in a room or more, but I don't think you can be very effective. My limit is 25 to 30 because I want to make sure I can have contact with each one of them. I want eye contact and one-on-one discussion with each person. If there are more than 30, I can't possibly meet and greet each one. Twenty-five to thirty seems to be the optimum number for us.

Silverman-ism:

Regret is worse than failure. In other words, not trying is much worse than trying and failing. I would rather try to get something done and fail than not even try at all—which is by definition defeat.

73

Pay Attention to Length

I have a small clock in the front of the room. I want to know what time we start and when we're getting close to being finished. I don't want to look at my wrist watch. I think that sends a bad signal, like maybe I'm getting bored or tired or just want to get out of there. When I want to monitor the time, I use a clock I can look at without looking down at my wrist.

I remember once watching former president Ronald Reagan when he was in a nationally televised debate. He kept looking at his watch. It sent the wrong message. It distracted him and distracted the viewers. He lost that debate. Was there a direct correlation between looking at his watch and losing the debate? I don't know, but I do know it did not look good. So I try to not let time be an obvious factor.

74

Using a Projector

I have my laptop set up and we use a screen. I can advance the slides with a wireless remote. I keep the laptop facing away from the audience and toward me. I stand off to the side of the screen so they can see the slides and I am not blocking them. I do this rather than walking in front of the audience and then turning my face to look at the slides. I don't want my back turned away from them.

I stand so I can see the laptop easily and maintain eye contact with the audience. I can just look down quickly to see where I am in my presentation. I will admit, not looking at my watch or paying attention to where I stand and not blocking their view are little things. But the devil is in the details. If you do all the details right, they add up. Most people would not even think about these things, but I believe you have to focus on all the details to have a successful workshop.

75

Give Everyone Name Tags as They Enter the Workshop

I give everyone a name tag. People love to hear their name and know you have made an effort to address them properly. And even though they are wearing a name tag, just calling someone by their first name always warms up my conversation with them. Plus, name tags will help your staff identify people who you might point out to them as important prospects.

We also discovered that the guests liked the name tags. It helps them interact and converse more freely with each other. The more fun they have, the more memorable the event. You want a free exchange of ideas to take place. The more engaged and interested they are the more questions you will get from them. This only serves to make the event more fun and entertaining.

76

Connect With the Audience

Once the main presentation is over, I work the room. I go around while people are still in their seats and talk to everyone I can meet. I often get asked personal questions that they didn't want to ask during the workshop.

Maria, who does all the workshops with me, has a list of everyone who attends. Sometimes I'll walk over to her while she is sitting at a table and say, "Maria that person over there is interested in x, y, or z; or, he is interested in knowing more about a, b, or c."

She starts making notes so when everyone leaves we know exactly what was important to everyone who said something significant. I try to draw them out so I can have a reason to see them.

77

Pass Out Materials

It is important to give them something tangible when they leave. We created the Silverman Financial brochure. It contains generic pieces with compliance-approved articles and facts. It discusses all of the advantages of working with a Certified Financial Planner.

I wrote a book on financial planning called—Financial Wisdom. I give everyone who comes into my office a copy. Having a book you have written is very effective and when you get to the point in your career when you think you have something worth publishing, I suggest you consider writing a book. It definitely helps gain the prospects' respect and can reinforce for them the advantages of financial planning and working with a credentialed advisor. All of which works to our advantage. None of my competitors have written a book, which separates us from the rest.

I also created customized pens to hand out. We give away markers, bookmarks, et cetera. We give out everything we can to promote ourselves in the workshops and help them remember us. Silverman Financial is all over these give-a-ways. We want to make it easier and more attractive for people to come in and see us.

78

Provide a Questionnaire

Here is another idea that we learned through trial and error. We created a questionnaire and on it we ask attendees about their hobbies, likes and dislikes. For example, someday in the future you can query your database and find out how many people say they like wine. So that will give you an opportunity to host a workshop focused on wine tasting. Imagine the response rate you'll get to invitations if you invite people who you know like wine!

Silverman-ism:

It isn't my job to motivate you. It's your job to motivate yourself. I can provide you with the tools and I can provide you with the ideas to help you reach whatever level you want to achieve, but you have got to do the work. You have to have the fire in your belly to do what others don't want to do. This will get you to where it is you ultimately want to go.

79

Get Guest Speakers Involved

At your special events, like the wine-tasting event, you might want to bring in a guest speaker who will talk about wine and conduct a wine-tasting opportunity. By bringing people together who have a common interest, it gives you a chance to network with attendees outside the normal parameters of a strictly business setting. What do you think the chances are you will find new business opportunities in this crowd of happy wine tasters?

80

Follow up with the Audience

On average, in a workshop of 30 people, we will get five or six appointments. Some people will come in and see us pretty quickly. What do we do with the rest of the people who came to the seminar but don't want to meet with us right now? My assistant is very good at following up and over time we might convert more than 60% of those people who were at that workshop. They will eventually come in and see us.

There are some authors who write books about how to conduct workshops and who brag about getting 90% of the attendees to make an appointment and to come in to see them. Well, maybe it is true. But based on our experience, those seminar speakers must be using something to entice the attendees into signing up. Otherwise, I just don't think that is realistic.

Besides, I don't like to pressure people. If they want to come in to see me, they'll come in; and if they don't, they won't. That has been my philosophy and it has worked for us. Pressure never pays off in the long run. In fact it can backfire.

I don't want to see people who have no real interest in taking action to improve their financial position. I'd rather have people come in who really do want to see us or at least have some interest in seeing us.

81

Be Different

I wanted to be a good public speaker. So I decided to hire a speech coach. The first thing he taught me was the importance of being different. He asked me what I liked to do when I was a child. I told him about being a professional magician.

He asked me if I was doing any magic in my workshops. I said no. He said "You need to start doing some." So I introduced this at the end of my workshop with a bag of colorful silk handkerchiefs.

I turn the bag inside out and I dump all the handkerchiefs out of the bag. The handkerchiefs are various colors. They are red, green and yellow. I hand them out to some of the people and say, "Folks, when people come into our office for their first meeting, I ask them to bring their updated financial statement. When I look at them, I find most people have money all over the place." Then I walk over and find a green handkerchief.

"You see this green handkerchief? It represents your cash that you have accumulated in your bank account. This red handkerchief right here represents that IRA you have. And this yellow handkerchief represents your Roth IRA."

I continue walking around. "And what happens is that when most people come in to see us, we take all of your statements, just like all of these handkerchiefs and we put them into our magic bag." Then I put all the handkerchiefs back into the magic bag and a moment later I pull out one solid scarf with all the colors mixed together like a rainbow! "This is the same way we help you organize your finances."

Then to prove that these are the same handkerchiefs, I turn the bag inside out showing that all the individual silk handkerchiefs are now gone. "If you come into our office with your finances in disarray and unsure of what to do or where you need to go to make things more organized, we'll help you. After we meet, you'll leave much better organized with a plan for retirement; you'll be able to see the whole picture. You'll know what you need to do to get from where you are to where you want to be."

That's how I close my workshop.

That's an example of being different, very different. It's something they remember and it's something I think is really effective in showing the value of how we work.

82

Compensate Your Staff for Helping at Workshops

One of the things I like to do with my staff is pay them based on results. The individual who works with me at the workshops earns a bonus for each person who attends. This is just another way to pay an incentive for a job well done.

When she gets back to the office all information we gathered is put into the computer. I keep a database of the attendees. We keep their contact information and anything we learn about them that is relevant. We give each of them a questionnaire to fill out during the workshop. I ask for their name, address, their e-mail address, whether they would like our complimentary newsletter, et cetera.

We track our results. It's funny, but we make more sales in years two and three than we do in year one. But we have to follow up. That extra effort pays off in the later years.

A Little Bit of Wisdom:

When a person applies enthusiasm to his job, the job will itself become alive with exciting new possibilities.

~ Norman Vincent Peale

83

Inject Humor Into Your Workshops

People like to laugh. So I also try to introduce some very basic humor into the workshop. I want them to know that I am not all business. Being all business intimidates some and turns off others. But I don't use too much humor, just enough to make the event more fun and entertaining.

84

Get Your Workshop Compliance Approved

I have mentioned this several times in different contexts, but I can't repeat it enough. Get your workshop compliance approved. That includes everything, whatever you pass out, your slides, fact sheets and even the basic script you plan to use.

I have been doing workshops for a long time. But even today, whenever we do a workshop, every single slide I put up on the screen has been brought to our compliance department for approval before we use them.

It has been said that the regulatory agencies are now showing up at workshops. It is like a Kmart shopper. They are there to see if I am complying. They want to see if I am misleading the attendees in any way. You've got to be very, very careful about what you do today and how you do it. Only use information and materials that are compliance approved.

85

How to Take Advantage of Continuing Education Requirements

You can earn a lot of brownie points by giving CE-approved seminars to attorneys and CPAs. They have to really scramble to earn continuing professional educational credits. When I figure out a topic I think is of interest and will qualify for continuing education credit, I will set up a seminar. This helps the attorneys and CPAs and helps me promote myself and get my name out there in front of people who are in a great position to refer business to me.

Create a workshop that is interesting and full of takeaways, handouts, slides, tables and tax citations, if possible. Make sure it complies with the continuing education rules so they can get credit. You have to take it to the professional licensing board in the state you work in. For example, let's say you're doing a workshop for Florida CPAs. You have to take your course material to the CPA board of the State of Florida and get the program approved.

You can then do the workshop, and at the end of it the professionals are credited with one or two hours (whatever the licensing board approves) of professional continuing education credit. Sometimes I'll even fly in an expert to make the presentation, in order to make the workshop even more attractive to potential attendees. And don't forget to get your workshop approved by your own compliance department.

The whole goal here is simple. You want to build a workshop that will stimulate interest in what you do in order to develop more business.

And, again, building a continuing education workshop is activity and nothing generates more business than activity. Remember this: activity leads to app-tivity. As my old friend See-More Sell-More says, "The more you see the more you sell." But you've got to get in front of people in order to make this happen and continuing education workshops are just one more way to get yourself out there and in front of potential clients and potential referrers.

86

Serve the Masses, Eat With the Classes

One of my heroes in the business, the late John Savage, used you say, "Serve the masses, eat with the classes. Serve the classes, and you'll go belly up."

What he meant by that was simply, seeing only super-rich people may help you succeed—but then again, you may not. Getting appointments with a lot of people greatly increases your odds of succeeding. Remember, there are more sparrows in the world than there are eagles. Activity breeds app-tivity. The harder you work, the luckier you become.

Little Bit of Wisdom:

There is no failure except in no longer trying. There is no defeat except from within, nor any really insurmountable barrier save our own inherent weakness of purpose.

~ Frank McKinney

87

Bring a Friend

One way to get more people into your workshops is to have everyone you invite bring a friend or two. Obviously, this increases the size of your audience. You need people to present to. They can't all be rich, but they can all have needs you can address and perhaps find a great solution.

88

Fewer but Better Qualified

In terms of having appointments, I believe you need to prequalify your appointments. It is far better to have fewer people—who are qualified to be clients come to see you—than having a lot of unqualified people come to see you and waste your time.

So you need a filter. This is why we have them fill out the questionnaire. It is a way for us to sort through the names and determine who is likely to be a good prospect. It is also why you want to meet the people during the seminar and determine whether you really want to work with them.

Build an inventory of names based on your criteria for quality prospects.

89

Key Ingredients for Sales

Now whenever you convert a workshop attendee into an office appointment, you've already got a lot of things going in your favor. Primarily, you have already met them once. They have seen you in a public setting and they usually have some kind of respect for you. This is important that they hold you in high esteem.

There are three ingredients for any sale. First, they have to know you. Then they have to like you and finally, they have to trust you. If you don't have all three of these, the odds of making a sale are slim to none.

When you do a workshop in a public setting, the attendees start to know you, like you and trust you.

90

Get Them Into Your Office

Just about all of our appointments from a workshop are scheduled for them to come into our office. Remember, we are targeting our workshops to specific markets—(like teachers, phone company employees, etc.). We do it on a basis of friends helping friends.

91

Make a Commitment

If you are going to do workshops, then you need to make a commitment to at least a one-year plan. You can't just decide that you are going to try it once or twice and then if it doesn't work out, decide to quit. It takes time to gain a foothold in the market.

You have to be committed with the financial resources for at least a year otherwise you shouldn't get into the business. What I discovered is you must continuously follow up with people who have attended your workshop. You must get their information into your database and then call them for appointments. You will have a much, much better chance of doing business with them if you work your system with discipline.

92

Sending Flyers

We have in our database at least 2500 names of people who have attended our workshops. We can tailor a mailing to our list of upcoming workshops. We design flyers that we distribute at the work site of our clients and prospects. Since many of them have been once, they may want to come again.

We're always marketing to our database as well as to new people. We always encourage them to bring along a friend.

Let's look at 2007. We did 25 workshops that year. A couple years later we were up to 40 workshops. We now do almost one a week. You can imagine how effective these workshops are or I wouldn't be investing so much time and money and effort into doing them. I cannot stress enough how important it is for you to learn how to use workshops as a way to create revenue and build your database.

A Little Bit of Wisdom:

When dealing with people, remember you are not dealing with creatures of logic, but creatures of emotion.

~ Dale Carnegie

93

Plan Workshops In Advance

Every January we map out our workshop schedule in advance. We plan exactly how many workshops we plan to do and where for the upcoming year. Within a week or two, we pretty much have them all set for the year. We may add some during the year, but only rarely will we eliminate any. My point is, we know where we're going almost as soon as a new year starts.

94

More on How to Sell Yourself through Workshops

The goal of a workshop is to sell you. That is your number-one goal. Your workshop is marketing, not selling. The goal of a workshop is for the attendees to want to do business with you. But to do this, you must convince them of the three elements of the sale. They must know you, like you and trust you as previously mentioned.

The "know you" occurs simply by them attending the workshop. Attendees spend an hour and a half with you, plus the dinner, getting to know you, your presentation style, your personality, your habits, your values. The whole point is to show that you are warm and approachable. Financial planning is terrifying for most people. A workshop encourages them to come in and see you.

I mentioned we use an IPRO in our seminars. This is our Independent Personal Retirement Overview. It is nothing more than a fancy name for our fact-finder.

I tell the folks, "There are two parts to our workshop. The first part is discussing your pension plan, your 401K, social security and what that all means to you. The second part of the workshop is helping you fill out our exclusive IPRO—our Independent Personal Retirement Overview. If you decide to come in to our office and meet with us, we will go through a very specific, customized planning session using this IPRO. It will help us know your situation and make specific recommendations that will help you answer the most important questions you are probably asking yourself."

What we need to do in this session is review these questions that most people have on their mind. "Can I afford to retire?" "Will I have an inflation hedge?" "Is my money going to be protected in a down market?" "Should I pay off credit card debt?" and "What's the best way to invest my money?"

Those are the things we will discuss in detail at one of our meetings. We do not charge a fee when they come in to see us. We just go through a planning session.

Think about it. You do a first meeting where you're marketing yourself to the public and then you do a second meeting where someone comes in to see you. It makes it a lot easier to meet qualified prospects compared to trying to call someone cold and then go out to an office and have a one-on-one.

95

Have the Home Field Advantage When You Have a Meeting

Who has the advantage in a football game, the home team or the visiting team? Most people say it is the home team. That is why I would rather have all my meetings in my office. I remember asking John Savage, one of the most respected MDRT members ever (and one of my heroes), "How do you get people to come into your office?"

Do you know what his answer was? "Ask them." It was that simple and it actually works. Even though you might think there would be resistance; many prospects agree to come in. And those who do come in are likelier to do business with us than if they let you come out to their home or place of business. They qualify themselves by showing they are serious enough to come to your office. It is that simple. Just ask them.

I tell my marketer to set up all of our meetings, or as many as she possibly can, in our office. I have a lot of meetings, because we meet a lot of people and you cannot make any sales unless you meet with them. I know I am stating the obvious, but it is worth mentioning again.

As an example, let's say that my goal is to get in front of 454 people during the course of a year (about nine people a week). Now, how many phone calls do I have to make in order to hold meetings with 454 different people? Well, from my metrics, I know if I pick up the phone and make phone calls I will ultimately get to meet with about one out of every three attempts I make for an appointment. These ratios are not cold calls, by the way. These are mostly calls to qualified leads, referrals, or follow-up calls.

Over time, my personal statistics show I would have to make about 1,029 phone calls to secure 454 appointments. Of course I won't get through to everyone I call, but I will get through to most of them. I know that sounds like a lot of phone calls, but in fact it is only 85 calls a month or about 25 calls a week. That's not unreasonable and if you are well organized, you can make all those calls in an hour or an hour and a half per day. But you must discipline yourself to do it.

It is a process that works by working the numbers. To me, numbers are king in selling. Work the numbers and your commissions will take care of themselves. After all, do you think the casinos in Las Vegas were built just on a whim? No. They have rooms full of actuaries who know exactly what someone is likely to spend in a casino. They know exactly how long someone will stay at a blackjack table or how much money someone will bet at the craps table in a casino. They know their numbers cold and we have to know ours as well.

I believe that in this business if you don't know your numbers cold, then you really shouldn't be in the business. That may sound harsh, but you are making it up as you go along. This business is the law of large numbers. You have to be willing to pay the price. But what is the price? Half of our business is all about really understanding the numbers side of financial planning. The other half is knowing your numbers.

Here is another thing about holding meetings in your own office. In the workshops I tell people, "We do not make house calls. We work from 8:00AM until 5:00PM. We don't work Saturdays or Sundays. If you want to come in and see us, fine. Maria, in my office, will call you to set up a meeting so we can go through your exclusive IPRO."

96

What are You Trying to Accomplish?

In any sales-related situation, you have to ask yourself, what is it that I'm trying to accomplish? It is also something you need to ask yourself when you're going into a meeting. When you are prospecting or conducting an interview with a client, you need a goal. "Start with the end in mind," as Stephen Covey wrote in his book, *Seven Effective Habits*. What is it you hope to get out of this?

What do you want to accomplish? I think too often, advisors go into meetings; having no clue what it is they want to have happen. As Yogi Berra said, "If you don't know where you want to go, you'll never get there." Keep that in mind. Know where you want to go and develop a plan to get there. Just get started. Do it with good planning and you'll reach your goal sooner than you think.

97

Where to Hold a Meeting

A little more about appointments: as I said, generally, all of our appointments are held in the office. We try to see about 100 people a month and I think if you hold the appointments in your office, you can use the home team advantage to increase your probability of success.

In our office, we have two financial advisors and we can effectively see 25 people each week without a problem. I can see three times as many people in my office compared to the number I can see if I go out their home or office. House calls, unless you have a highly qualified prospect or a very special situation, are not worth it.

If you're traveling to someone else's office, you have to deal with traffic and parking. You have to contend with directions and not getting lost. You have the possibility of someone potentially not even being there. This all takes time away from what you could be doing if you stayed in your office. Your productively will suffer if you have to go out of your office for meetings.

Because of our process, we have very, very few cancellations. It is not that we do not have any, don't get me wrong, but not a lot, because we have someone whose job it is to follow up to make sure the people are coming to our office as planned.

If we make an appointment and someone doesn't show up to my office it's not like I have downtime. I have other things I can do. However, the person who does all my appointment setting actually confirms every appointment, just like a doctor's office would. We call them as a reminder the day before and make sure they know how to get to our office. This increases our appointment rate significantly.

98

Make It a Comfortable Environment

When I speak to advisor groups I am asked what type of table and desk arrangement I have in my office. Is it a rectangular old-fashioned table or is it a round table?

I think there is a big difference in the two tables. When I grew up, my father was the head of the household. Guess who sat at the head of the table? My father did and everyone else sat around him at the table.

I did not want a set up like this in my office. So we designed our offices with round tables. We do not want anyone to be perceived as sitting at the head of the table. I want to give the impression to our prospects and clients that they are in control. They can sit anywhere they want. It gives them a sense of confidence and that is important and what I desire.

So, try to have a round table. There is no head of the table. No one is the boss. It is just a meeting of equals discussing important topics.

Once a client arrives, we spend as much time as it takes to get to know them, but as quickly as possible. We will get right into the fact-finding process so we can figure out how we can best help them.

Everyone in my office knows most of our clients. So when they walk in, it is like a family environment where we really try to greet them and make them feel at ease. If they are a new prospect from a seminar, we give them the family treatment.

I mentioned before that we try to know what kind of coffee or tea they like, that kind of thing. It really does make a big difference. Not only do they appreciate the beverage of their choice, they notice how efficient we are, and it helps give them confidence in us. Again, it's the little details that count.

99

Decorating Your Office

Another important aspect to our office is how it looks. The insurance world is famous for handing out all kinds of plaques, memorabilia and awards. I should know. I have about 70 of them. But they are in my house, in the attic. I used to proudly display all of these plaques and awards as a way to show we were successful. But over time they began to lose their meaning. I realized you don't spend plaques and awards or accolades. You can only retire with the money you earn every day.

None of the plaques or awards are displayed in my office. What is displayed in my office are pictures of trips my wife and I have taken to South Africa, of beautiful landscapes, wild animals—things like that. We have artwork from local artists too. My wife and I have had the good fortune of traveling all over the world and have photographs and things we collected from those trips. I display the artwork and crafts my success has brought me.

Plaques, in my opinion, are really for your own ego gratification. They have nothing to do with the public and the public really could care less if you were the premium leader one year or one month. The public cares about how you can help them. By displaying the symbols of your own success, they see tangible evidence you can help them succeed too. After all, they don't want to help you become a premium leader. They want to retire and travel around the world. So show them you can do that for them.

I would suggest you get rid of the plaques and get more pictures and artwork in your office. Another thing we've done is to display pictures of my wife and my daughter in the office. I love my wife and my daughter and I want people to know I really am a family-oriented person. They can see that and then they often ask me questions which ultimately circles back to financial planning.

A Little Bit of Wisdom:

When you are tough on yourself, life is going to be easier on you.

~ *Zig Ziglar*

100

Display Thank-You Letters

When clients walk into your office and they're in your waiting room, what do they typically see? Normally you will see a Wall Street Journal, a local newspaper, a brochure or pamphlet. We don't have any of these in our office. I don't allow it.

What we do have is a collection of thank-you letters from clients. I probably have 60 or 70 thank-you notes from clients expressing how happy they were with our services and how much it helped them. They have been sent to us and we have three books of them in our waiting area. The only thing our clients can read while they wait, is what is in those books. That is all we have for them to see. And, of course, I have a copy or two of Financial Wisdom—the book that I wrote.

I have noticed almost everyone picks up one of those books and flips through it. It is very subtle marketing, but it shows what a great job we do for clients. It is also an effective way to demonstrate client satisfaction. So make sure you never discard or file away a thank-you note. Put it to good use in your waiting room.

I purposely have people wait four or five minutes before I will see them. I want them to pick up one of the thank-you books. If they are not on their cell phone, they will pick up the book that is sitting in the waiting area and they will read what other people have written about us.

101

Dress Code

What's the dress code in your office? I believe you should look professional in your attire. I no longer wear ties in my office because of the South Florida culture. However I wore a suit to work every day for 25 years.

Recently I have learned to dress down a little more. I don't wear a tie to work, but, again, this depends on what part of the country you are in and what is the commonly accepted practice in your region. In New York City, for example, I would imagine most people wear a suit and tie.

In my town, Miami, it is an accepted practice to dress down and that even goes for a lot of the big firms in the downtown area as well.

102

Give Clients Things They Like

Prior to the days when I displayed the thank-you note collections, we had a selection of books out front—books clients were likely to be interested in reading. Books that might be of interest to someone when he or she retires, like a book on gardening, golf, art or whatever it is. We bought a bunch of these books from Amazon.com and put those out front in the waiting area.

My staff was trained to notice which books clients picked up and then later when they were leaving the office, we would give them the book they had been looking at. Invariably, a client or prospect would say, "Oh no, I can't take that. But we would say, "Please. Take it. By all means, it's all yours. You obviously have an interest in that, so please let me give it to you." Ninety percent of the people would take it. Then, every time they would see that book, part of their brain would think of us. Again, a book doesn't cost that much, but it's an invaluable marketing tool.

103

Bake Cookies

Another thing we do is bake cookies. We noted where they make the cookies you find in the first-class section of plane. The ones I like the most are made by Otis Spunkmeyer. We called the company and bought one of their baking ovens. We buy a lot of their cookie dough and store it in our freezer in the office. We make fresh cookies every morning.

You may ask, "Well, what does that have to do with marketing? Everything. The smell of fresh-baked cookies each day is there to give our visitors a sense of family.

I knew the idea was working when one day a client called me back and said, "Okay, I'll come to see you at your office, but only if I can have a dozen cookies." I told her "of course" and the next afternoon she showed up as planned. I made a large sale, and some of the credit goes to a couple of bucks' worth of Otis Spunkmeyer cookies. The idea really does work.

Who would have ever imagined a plateful of cookies would distinguish us from the competition? Again, you want to separate yourself from the rest of the pack.

104

The Audio Business Card

Another marketing technique we have developed is an audio business card. Now keep in mind this must be compliance approved. A number of years ago we developed an audio business card. It has a picture of me on the front of the card and when you open it up it plays a five-or six-minute audio of what Certified Financial Planners do and how they can help. I passed a lot of these out and they worked. We actually got a lot of calls from people for appointments.

Keep in mind that almost any kind of marketing works, as long as you are willing to work. Over time you will notice what works best compared to what works only so-so. But almost any marketing effort will succeed to some extent if you work it. Many will invest in marketing ideas, but then they don't work them. If you do this, you have wasted your time and money. But more important, you have lost business to some competitor.

Find something you like and do it and then keep working it. Never give up. You may try something today and get no results. Then, two years from now, someone may call you and say, "I remember a workshop you held a couple of years ago and I still have that great marker pen you handed out. That's why I still have your name and phone number. I'd like to come in and talk to you." You would be surprised at how well these simple little ideas really work.

105

Love Affair Marketing

Love affair marketing is really going out of your way to really make clients feel special. One thing you can do to make clients feel special is to send fruit gift baskets. Based on compliance regulations you have to limit how much money you spend, but you can still do things like gift baskets. You just can't go overboard. Check with your company's compliance department first.

When someone we know is retiring, we will send a small gift basket to their place of business one week before they are scheduled to leave the job.

We do this at their place of business because we want everyone else to see it and come by their desk and say, "Wow, who did you get that from?" We want them to say, "Oh, it was from Silverman Financial." That's the whole point. It generates conversation around a potential client and creates word-of-mouth buzz. That is an example of love affair marketing.

106

Network Your Clients

Another thing you can do is to network your clients together. You may wonder what that has to do with marketing. It has a lot to do with marketing. Here's an example.

I was referred to a potential client who had a disabled child. The woman came in to see me and said, "My husband, unfortunately, died in the hospital recently and we think the doctor may have messed up."

I know quite a few personal injury attorneys. I was able to refer the woman to one my clients, who happens to be one of the best personal injury attorneys in town. She liked him and hired him. I don't know where this case will end up, but that's networking your clients together. It makes them feel good about what you're doing for them, and instead of one happy client, I now have two happy clients (one who may refer others to me) and a powerful attorney who is also in a position to refer a lot of business as well. The next time that attorney has someone who might benefit from my services, do you think he'll refer his client to another agent? Or to me, the guy who did him a favor. It's great and everybody wins. Me, the attorney, and most importantly, the client.

107

Referral Sources

Are you marketing yourself to bankers, estate planning attorneys and CPAs? I get together with estate planning attorneys, CPAs, and bankers as often as I can. I would never just meet with them for some self-serving purpose. I always bring a new creative idea with me.

A major part of our business is to stay in front of people. If you are not in front of people, you have no chance of them thinking about you when the next referral client comes their way. You have to motivate them to think of you when a referral opportunity arises.

So I would say this is a marketing strategy. If you wanted to really do more business with wealthy people, you might market yourself to one hundred CPA's during the next year. If you see two a week, you will have seen one hundred over the course of the year. You take them to lunch. You share a hot new idea or concept with them. You tell them things other insurance or financial planning professionals failed to tell them. This distinguishes you from the rest of the pack.

You want to think about the following when you see them, what can I do to enhance their business?" Remember, you can get whatever you want if you help people get what they want first. If I don't go see them, they are not thinking about how they can help enhance my business. What I have to do is tell them how I can become a source of referrals to them.

You never know how the chemistry is going to work with that CPA. But if you see one hundred CPAs annually, eighty of them won't even bother with you again. But twenty will. Twenty may send you a little bit of business and maybe ten of them will send you a lot of business. But you've got to be able to work a game plan and market yourself effectively in order to make this happen.

And in this example, working your game plan means getting a list of CPAs in your area and calling on them and inviting them out to lunch. Many will turn you down, but many will take you up on your offer. And when that happens, you have created an amazing opportunity for yourself, practically out of thin air.

108

Make Thank-You Calls and Send Thank-You Letters

Here is another thing I do. A client, whose retirement plan I set up, referred a new person to us. The prospect came in for his meeting. After I completed my appointment with him, I picked up the phone and called the referring client. I said, "Joe, I just want to let you know that so and so came in to see me this afternoon and agreed to have us set up his retirement plan. I want to thank you for referring him to us and for helping him get into our office. We are going to treat him with kid gloves and provide first-class service as you would expect. But I really wanted to thank you for thinking of me."

If you would rather send a note than make a call, that's great too. Just make sure you acknowledge the referrer one way or another. It's very important and it is polite. Plus, it helps the referrer think of you when future opportunities arise.

109

Remember Their Birthdays

Birthday cards and phone calls are hard wired into our database system. We love birthdays. What I do is call clients on the phone. For example, I might say, "Hi Charlie, I just want to wish you a happy birthday today. Just thinking about you and I hope everything is great." I never try to sell anything during this call. I just want to say hello.

Some sales people send out e-mail birthday cards, but how many take the time to make a phone call? Not many. This is another detail that makes us different from the rest. Remember, the key to marketing is to make yourself a little different from everyone else. Just calling to try to make a sale to someone is not marketing.

These birthday calls generally are done first thing in the morning or at the very end of the day. If I get someone's voice mail, I don't really care because it is the effort that counts. The fact that I called, whether I connect or leave a message, is all that matters. I just want them to hear my voice.

110

More About Birthday Phone Calls

I wish I could tell you that we connect with each one of our clients on their birthday. But we don't. I try to look at the database to see who has a birthday on a given day. I try to pick up the phone and call that person to wish them a happy birthday. I cannot call them all. But we do reach a lot of them. What is important is trying to stay in touch with clients on a personal level over and above just calling them for an appointment for an annual review. And it seems to work.

As I mentioned, I recently made a pretty good sale over the phone. Just by making the call. This one sale was to a woman in Atlanta. I had never met her, but I had her in my database. I called to wish her a happy birthday and she said, "You know, I just retired last week and I invested my money with someone else."

Well it turned out she never did invest her money with anyone else, she just thought she had. I helped her discover her money was just sitting in a money market account with another advisor. She was coming down to Florida for her retirement party and I invited her into the office. I was able to see her face to face and subsequently was able to invest $230,000 from her retirement. So birthday phone calls work really well. If you have a database management system like we use, EZ Data, you can pull up everyone with a birthday on any given day and then make phone calls to wish them a happy birthday. As a matter of fact, any reason at all that you can find to contact a client or prospective client is something you should always do. That's an activity that seems to always pay off handsomely.

111

CardWare

For years, I used to sign all the birthday cards. Now we use something called CardWare which, again, has been approved by the broker/dealer. I have one of my assistants take my handwriting and convert it into a font. Now we can write a customized message in my handwriting for a birthday card. We send this out instead of doing it by hand each month. And because there is a sample of every letter in the alphabet, CardWare can make it look like I actually wrote out the entire card by hand. What a time-saver and it makes keeping in touch with clients and prospects a lot easier.

I had a Christmas party last year and one of my employees sent me a thank-you note for the party. I had no idea that it came from CardWare. It looked amazingly personal. I would have sworn she handwrote it. I was absolutely floored when I saw the card and realized software made it happen.

112

Advertise Yourself

Pens and markers are commonplace, but still very important. I had pens created with "Silverman Financial" and all of our contact information on it, including our tagline: "Even though you've retired, your money doesn't have to."

We give them away to everyone who comes in the office. We have highlight markers we give away too. I'm giving those out all the time, and again, just to get our name out there. We have note pads with "Silverman Financial" on it and another tag line: "Proud to be your financial planner."

We have also developed bookmarks and pads of paper we give away to people. We've recently started to use chip clips with our name prominently displayed on it. I just bought 1500 of these clips and I am ready to order more. You have to keep promoting yourself every way you can think of. It all adds up, believe me.

113

Market Through Your Web Site

Another way to do marketing is through your Web site. How are you doing to promote yourself on the Internet? Once again, you have to be very careful about this because of the compliance laws concerning what you can and cannot say.

What we did was rather than developing our own custom Web site which the regulators would have turned down, I simply went to my broker/dealer and asked, "Is there an existing Web site out there you would approve? We could model ours after it and not risk violating compliance rules.

In a nutshell, the answer was yes and today we use a shell template for our Web site. The concept has already been approved by compliance, all we do is customize it and add approved content. Then we have our own customized site for the entire world to see.

In other words, rather than spending a lot of money to custom-create a Web site that compliance might likely not allow, all you need to do is to go to your broker/dealer and ask them for examples of Web sites that are approved. Doing this will save you lots of time and money.

114

Ice Cream Day and Picnic

Another marketing technique is something that I call ice cream day. We'll rent an ice cream truck and keep it out front of the office so people will come down and get ice cream. It is really popular (remember we're in South Florida) and once people show up, we hand out flyers for an upcoming workshop.

Another way to market is to get yourself involved with the unions within the larger companies you have access to in your area. We are very well networked with the presidents of the local unions. We do everything we can think of to help them, because they really, in turn, help us.

Again, I suggest you get involved in the financial services industry, be it the MDRT, NAIFA, IAFP or any other industry-related organization, because the more involved you are, the more marketing ideas you will pick up. Remember, marketing brings you suspects, suspects bring you prospects, and prospects bring you applications. As I've said, "activity creates apptivity."

Silverman-ism:

If you do more than you are paid to do, one day you will be paid more than you actually do.

115

Employee Handbook

In my office, I use an employee handbook. Each employee must sign this when they begin working at Silverman Financial. It's about 70 pages. It details our policies. Like, what happens in the event of a hurricane, how many days off they are allowed per year and what hours they are to work. It's a very detailed manual. In addition, we have a do-not-compete clause. Why do I take such steps? Well, I have built a very good business model and I don't want someone coming in and learning from me and then taking that model out into the outside world and trying to duplicate it against us.

A Little Bit of Wisdom

Be cautious when others are greedy and be greedy when others are cautious.

~ *Warren Buffett*

116

Annual Client Reviews

Annual client reviews, in my opinion, are the key to keeping your business on the books.

You don't necessarily have to have people come in to your office to hold an annual review. You might have a client who is fully invested, so seeing them in your office and spending time with them each year really isn't productive in generating additional new sales, so to speak. So just do it over the phone. You would be surprised by what you learn. You might even find out they got an inheritance or came into a sum of money. It pays to call.

117

Always Keep In Contact

Of course, you should keep in touch with clients in case they need anything or in case their situation changed. But in terms of generating new business, spending time with them is not productive. Usually it is best to have someone on your staff do this kind of contact work. Also, keeping in contact provides an opportunity to ask for referrals.

You don't lose clients as much when you make it your company's practice to always stay in touch with clients. Make sure you follow up with them. That's something you really need to do consistently. Make sure you have a process to handle this. There should be a process in place for everything you do in your office.

A Little Bit of Wisdom

I've missed more than 9,000 shots in my career. I've lost almost 300 games. On 26 occasions, I've been entrusted to take the game winning shot and missed. I failed over and over and over again in my life and that's why I succeed.

~ Michael Jordan

118

Prospecting Via CD Due Dates

I mentioned this before, but in case you forgot, it bears repeating. Ask, "When does your next CD come due?" You probably have a lot of people who have several CDs. You can train your office staff to ask clients when it comes due so they can plug that date into the database and they can pull it up in a timely manner. You then call your client and inform them their CD is coming due on such-and-such a date. Most of time you will have a new sale. You also have something to talk to them about, something that you can do for them.

119

It Doesn't Always Go Right

Does everything you do or try to do go well all the time? No, absolutely not. But things do go well most of the time and that's what you should strive for. For example, what do you call a batter who fails to get on base two out of every three times at bat? You call him a Hall-of-Famer. Getting on base once out of three at-bats means you're hitting .333—and who hits better than that? So, you can strike out plenty of times and it doesn't matter. What matters is how well you do when you are hitting.

120

Dictation Services

We use a service called CopyTalk. This is a telephone service that will transcribe client notes over the phone. I dictate what I want to remember. Then they transcribe the notes and send them back to me via e-mail. When these notes get sent back to me, I edit every page to make sure it's exactly what I want. Then it gets e-mailed to all of the office staff and is posted to their SmartPad computerized note-keeping system. Each set of notes is tagged so anyone calling or looking up that client will know exactly what was discussed during the last meeting.

> **Silverman-ism:**
>
> **If you don't try you're not going to succeed and if you don't step up to bat there's no chance to succeed.**

121

How I Do It

Based on ideas from my strategic coach, I've learned to focus on the top 20 business relationships. We call these our client opportunities. These are the ones you think you can earn significant income from over the next 90 days.

This list is what ultimately pays the bills. I told you about my farm club. They are the next 20 relationships I am in the process of developing, my hope for the future. At all times we are working with 40 relationships. That alone can keep you busy, but it's not enough. That's why I urge you to perfect your prospecting and referral skills.

I keep my eye on the ball. I have a goal as to what amount of revenue we need for any given quarter. And as we pay for business, that gets subtracted from the goal-to-go list. My goal is to meet that objective every quarter. We are always close if not exceeding it.

The key is my top 20 relationships. My goal starts each quarter by reviewing the list of top 20 relationships that I think I can pay for during the next 90 days. In other words, I am constantly updating the list every week. When I sell someone on the list, I have to replace them from the farm team. And when that happens, I need to put someone on the farm team to take their place. When we get to the end of December, my new goal for the next year will be based on my remaining top 20 relationships. I might have 40 things I am working on at any point in time. But I want to keep a close eye on those 20 top relationships because those are the most important opportunities I have.

In school, it was obvious on any given test that one question might be worth more than another one. One question might only be worth one point, but there was another question that was worth fifteen points. But if you were struggling with that one one-point question you could waste your entire test time on it. So you had to forget it and move on.

Well, that same theory applies to our business. You want to spend your time where you can make the most money. My to-do list focuses on all those people whom I have to follow-up with in a short time frame. I have a list of people who have given me referrals. I also keep a list of what I call my accounts receivable, which is the name of the person, the premium, the net commission, the date we wrote it, the company, whether I picked up the check or not, the status of the case and whether or not it has been approved.

With a system like this, I am incredibly well organized and I know where my business is at all times. If you don't run your business as a business, you run the risk of failing. You must stay organized.

122

Know Your Revenues and Expenses

Do you know what your revenues are? Do you have a profit and loss statement? Do you know your expense ratios? I know exactly and I know, for example, my overhead runs about 25% to 30% of my gross revenues. So about 70% of what comes to Silverman Financial is profit to me. Have you figured out your profit ratios?

123

Know Your Ratios

If you know your ratios then you know what you have to do in order to make things work. As I mentioned earlier in this book, you must know how many calls you have to make and how many noes you are going to get to how many yeses you're going to get and how many cancellations you're going to get and how many people you're going to actually see.

If you know your closing ratio, then you know how many people you must see in order to know how many are going to buy. And if you know your average sales, you know exactly what you're going to earn. If you go to work and work your plan each day, your goal will actually be achieved by the end of the year, if not sooner.

Silverman-ism:
Ordinary people do an extraordinary job in order to get to the next level.

124

Read Books by Motivational Speakers

If you want to read a book to help you sell, you will want to read a book by a well-known motivational speaker. If you want to know how to achieve in business, read a book from someone who is actually getting it done day to day, not just someone who is in the business of speaking for fees. You want to read books by people who are walking their walk, not merely talking the talk.

My belief is you always want to seek out people who are actually succeeding in the financial services business. I want to know how someone is getting done the same exact thing I am trying to do. I don't care about the selling techniques of someone who is selling magazine subscriptions or Rolls Royces. I want to read books by motivational speakers who are selling financial services.

I want to know they are actually doing it, in other words, being successful in what it is they're doing and not just talking about it. I don't need to hear from someone who is telling me how to do it—without having actually done it.

125

Get Going!

The ideas, techniques and strategies I've shared with you in *Proven Ways To The Top* are the same ones I have been using to bring me great success over the years. If you noticed, they are not profound. Quite the contrary, they are simple. But I know they can catapult you to the next level. The rest is up to you. Are you willing to take it to the next level? Do you have the burning desire to make it happen? Remember 10 little words with no more than 2 syllables, "If it is to be, it is up to me."

I've given you the ingredients, but it's up to you to make the stew. You have to put them all together to make a fabulous feast for yourself. And that takes work—hard work—but you do not need extraordinary talents to achieve extraordinary selling. All you need to do is have a plan and work it consistently. If you do that, the results will take care of themselves.

Good luck, and if you have any questions or comments, please don't hesitate to get in touch with me personally at 305-670-7088, or e-mail me at marc@sfinancial.com.

Best of luck!

—Marc Silverman

APPENDIX

Month of December

DATE	PLACE	NEW	CLIENT	PREMIUM	COMM.	TYPE	COMPANY

The page you are looking at is titled the Month of December. I create one of these charts for each month of the year.

This is how I track every sale that I make in a given month. I indicate the date that the case was sold, whether it was placed or not, whether it was new or old, the name of the client, the premium, the commission, the type of sale, and the insurance company that it is placed with.

Month of December (Cont.)

On the bottom of this page I add up my numbers as to what I have done during the month, and then I total what was done for the year-to-date, including my investment commissions, my first-year commissions, and my total commissions, the annuity premium, the investment dollars, the life premium, and total premium.

TOTAL WRITTEN

	MTD	YTD
Investment Lives		
MDRT Lives		
Total Lives		

Investment Commission		
1st Year Commission		
Total Commission		

Annuity Premium		
Investment Dollars		
Life Premium		
Total Premium		

The reason I accumulate these numbers is so that I know how I am doing during the year, and as the old expression goes, "winners keep score and losers do not." There is no way to better yourself unless you are keeping score of what you are actually doing. So I encourage you to use this or something similar to this in order to track your own numbers and your own production.

Tracking Numbers

Week of:	Calls Made	Appts. Made From Calls	Appts. Made To Start Week	Appts. Kept	Pocket-Books New	G or I	Actual Lives	Written 1st Year Comm.
5-Jan								
12-Jan								
19-Jan								
26-Jan								
Monthly Totals								
2-Feb								
9-Feb								
16-Feb								
23-Feb								
Monthly Totals								
1-Mar								
8-Mar								
15-Mar								
22-Mar								
29-Mar								
Monthly Totals								
5-April								
12-April								
19-Aprl								
26-April								
Monthly Totals								
3-May								
10-May								
17-May								
24-May								
31 May								
Monthly Totals								
7-Jun								
14-Jun								
21-Jun								
28-Jun								
Monthly Totals								
5-Jul								
12-Jul								
19-Jul								
26-Jul								
Monthly Totals								

Tracking Numbers (Cont.)

Week of:	Calls Made	Appts. Made From Calls	Appts. Made To Start Week	Appts. Kept	Pocket-Books New	G or I	Actual Lives	Written 1st Year Comm.
2-Aug								
9-Aug								
16-Aug								
23-Aug								
30-Aug								
Monthly Totals								
6-Sep								
13-Sep								
20-Sep								
27-Sep								
Monthly Totals								
4-Oct								
11-Oct								
18-Oct								
25-Oct								
Monthly Totals								
1-Nov								
8-Nov								
15-Nov								
22-Nov								
29-Nov								
Monthly Totals								
6-Dec								
13-Dec								
20-Dec								
27-Dec								
Monthly Totals								

This is how I was able to develop my statistics over time. I wanted to know how many calls I needed to make in order to get a given number of appointments during the week. Each week I would track the number of phone calls I actually made, how many appointments I made from these calls, how many appointments I made to start the week and how many appointments were actually kept. How many appointments were kept versus how many appointments I made to start the week would show me my cancellation ratio during the week. If I knew I had to make 100 calls to get 13 appointments then it's very easy to know how many calls I need to make a day in order to get the appointments that I want to make. More appointments, more sales.

Everything starts with appointments. Once you figure out how many phone calls you need to make to get these appointments the rest is quite easy. I also kept track of my new pocketbooks. New pocketbooks refers to the number of people that actually purchased from me. If a husband and wife purchase from me, this is considered 1 pocketbook, not 2. It is suggested that we have no fewer than 50 new pocketbooks a year so I always strive for at least this. G and I on this page stands for group or individual. I also keep track of the written first-year commissions. This is totaled up each week and at the end of the year I know my numbers very much like a casino does.

Income Goals For 2010

Source	Weekly	Monthly	Yearly
Override	$	$	$
Trails/Renewals	$	$	$
Group Commission	$	$	$
1st Year Commission–All Companies	$	$	$
Other	$	$	$
	$	$	$

How To Accomplish This

Based on weeks (42)

Source	Weekly	Monthly	Yearly
Lives	$	$	$
I must see	$	$	$
I make the following	$	$	$
I must dial on phone	$	$	$

To Meet 2010 Goal Average Commission/Case $__________________

2009 Statistics Based on First-Year Commission of $_________________

I worked approximately 192 days or 38 weeks in 2009

Each call was worth $ __________

Each appointment kept was worth $ _____________

Each sale was worth $ _______________

Closing ratio equals _______%

Cancellation ratio was _______%

People seen in average month = _______

Average number of appointments/week = _______

I make ____% of appointments on the phone

Of appointments made, approximately ______% on phone and _____% in field

Income Goals For 2010 (Cont.)

The previous page is titled Income Goals For 2010. As you can see, I like to know where my income is coming from and what the game plan is to make this happen. The first thing I do is write down the source of where the money is going to come from. I break it down yearly, monthly, and weekly, and then I write down how to actually accomplish this based on 42 work weeks during the year because of time I take off for vacation and industry activities.

Based on my 2009 statistics, I know that I must dial on the phone 1,029 times in order to sell 200 lives. So, if you walk into your office and you know that for every time you pick up the phone, you make $500, my question to you is how many times would you pick up the phone? In this example I also used my 2009 statistics based on a given level of first-year commissions to figure out the numbers which will generate business for the given year. For example, I know that I worked 192 days or 38 weeks in '09, I know how much each call is worth, how much each appointment kept was worth, each sale, my closing ratio, my cancellation ratio, and the people seen in an average month. This is all great information in order to help you get to the next level. If you know your numbers, this is half the battle.

2010 Goals

EXISTING INCOME

Accounts Receivable		$
Trails/Renewals	$	
Group		$

INCOME RANGES

Conservative	
Total First-Year Commission–All Companies	$
Existing Income	$

Realistic	
Total First-Year Commission–All Companies	$
Existing Income	$

Aggressive	
Total First-Year Commission–All Companies	$
Existing Income	$
	$

There is another page I utilize within goal setting titled 2010 Goals. Please refer to the top of this page where it says existing income. This is the income that I have coming in to my company before the year starts. It helps to know this, it helps with budgeting for the year.

I have developed three income ranges, conservative, realistic, and aggressive, and I always target my overall goal to my aggressive each year. I want to know ranges of income from conservative to realistic to aggressive and then of course I target to the aggressive goal.

What I Need In 2010

Expense	Monthly	Annual
Home	$	$
Office	$	$
Taxes @ 30%	$	$
Simple IRA	$	$
	$	$

SAVINGS GOAL 2010

	Goal	Achieved
401(k)	$	$
Simple Ira	$	$
Interest Income	$	$
Life Insurance Capital	$	$
Growth in Pension	$	$
	$	$

Lastly, there is what I need in 2010. I want to know what I need to bring in in a given year in order to keep all of the "balls" in the air. So, for example, how much do I need to satisfy my home expenses? How much does it cost to run the office, my taxes, and money going into a pension plan? This lets me know what I need to bring in annually. In addition, I set savings goals for the year and I would suggest that each of you follow a similar methodology in order to know your numbers.